Media,
Communication,
Culture

Media, Communication, Culture

A Global Approach

James Lull

Columbia University Press
New York

Columbia University Press
New York   Chichester, West Sussex
Copyright © 1995 James Lull

Library of Congress Cataloging-in-Publication Data available
on request

ISBN: 0–231–10264–X
ISBN: 0–231–10265–8 (pbk.)

First published in the U.K. by Polity Press, Cambridge, in
association with Blackwell Publishers.

∞

This book is printed on acid-free paper

Printed and bound in Great Britain

c 10 9 8 7 6 5 4 3 2 1
p 10 9 8 7 6 5 4 3 2 1

Contents

Acknowledgements

Many people help you in many ways to write a book. This is especially true here because, as I point out in the introduction which follows, I have been working on this volume for a long, long time. Some people have helped me close to home; others from a distance. Some of these people are family and friends; others are known to me only through their published work. The acknowledgements pages give me a chance to mention family and friends; the names of others permeate the text.

Books always signify something important in the author's personal history too. My mother, Verna Marie Lull, passed away during the period when I was completing the book. Verna's strength, sensitivity, intelligence, and beauty have inspired me in all my undertakings.

I have had several good colleagues at the two institutions where I have taught in California the past 20 years. I especially wish to thank Jim Bradac and Harvey Molotch at the University of California, Santa Barbara, and Dave Elliott, Serena Stanford, Phil Wander, and Tim Hegstrom at San José State University. Guillermo Orozco Gómez, Klaus Bruhn Jensen, Dave Morley, Karl Erik Rosengren, Marsha Siefert, Leoncio Barrios, Ien Ang, Marcia Terlaje-Salas, Stefanie Izumi, Toshie Takahashi Sato, Debbie Johnson, and Frank García have all contributed something important and unique to the book. My work has also benefited from discussions with Ulf Hannerz, Ingunn Hagen, Juha Kytömäki, Zhang Li-fen, Michael Marx, and Steve Hinerman. Trish Marinas, Kim Pham, and Stefanie Izumi created the graphics. My friends and colleagues in Brazil made 1992 a very meaningful and productive year for me. Eduardo Neiva and Heloisa Aguiar were with me every step of the way in Rio, and then some. Rita Marques and Ana Paula Mandina of TV Globo in Rio kindly assisted me at the network archive. I also wish to thank Agnes da Silva, Tomas Pereira, Everardo Rocha, Ronaldo Hellal, Maria Claudia Coelho, Maria Immacolata Vassalo Lopes, Renata Veloso, Angeluccia Habert, and the wonderful Fulbright Commission staff in Rio de Janeiro, especially Nilza Waldeck, Marisa Leal, and Rita Monteiro.

I am extremely pleased with the professional relationship I have developed with Polity Press, originating publishers of this book, over the past few years. The entire staff has been wonderful. But I am most deeply indebted to John B. Thompson who somehow manages not only to teach sociology at Cambridge University and write extraordinary books, but also to serve as editor for Polity Press. Professor Thompson's work *Ideology and Modern Culture* is one of the foundation references upon which my analyses and commentaries rest. John B. Thompson supervized development and publication of this manuscript with meticulous professionalism and warm personal attention. Thanks in no small measure to him, I found writing this book to be a very rewarding experience.

James Lull
San Francisco

Introduction

Like people, books sometimes take long and curious journeys. This one surely has. I began researching and writing this book in Lund, Sweden in the summer of 1981, although at the time I had absolutely no idea that the work I was doing in Scandinavia would finally resemble what appears in this volume. Influenced by countless books, conversations, and trips to many countries and cultures during the intervening years, I have revised, revised, and revised again what appears in the following pages. In fact, one incarnation or another of this manuscript has been kicking around in my files and on my desk as a kind of personal working document about media, communication, and culture for most of my academic career. The book has grown with the times. The perspective represented in this writing reflects the key epistemological shift in the recent intellectual history of the social sciences – a decisive turn away from logical positivism, its universalist assumptions and pretenses toward theoretical and empirical questions of culture and meaning and the use of qualitative research methodologies. Consequently, much of today's theorizing is far more bold and interesting than what we have seen in previous years. We now more fully recognize in communication and cultural studies what Clifford Geertz saw in the more entrenched social science disciplines in the early 1980s:

Ten years ago the proposal that cultural phenomena should be treated as significative systems posing expositive questions was a much more alarming one for social scientists – allergic, as they tend to be, to anything literary or inexact – than it is now. In part, it is a result of the growing recognition that the established approach to treating such phenomena, law-and-causes physics, was not producing the triumphs of prediction, control, and testability that had for so long been promised in its name. And, in part, it is a result of intellectual deprovincialization. The broader currents of modern thought have finally begun to impinge upon what has been, and in some quarters still is, a snug and insular enterprise. (1983: 3)

After numerous jaunts to parts of the world that intrigue me most, especially Latin America and the Far East, I recently had an opportunity to spend a year in Rio de Janeiro, Brazil, where I taught (on a very relaxed schedule!) at the Catholic University and the State University of Rio de Janeiro. With the distinct advantages of interesting friends and colleagues, beautiful weather and beaches, the largest dance floor in South America, and a sustained period to read and concentrate on a wide range of relevant material – much of it written by Latin American scholars – I was able to finally complete several chapters of this book. One can have a unique perspective on culture and communication from a place like Brazil. And the timing was fortunate. While I was there Brazil hosted a controversial world congress on ecology and underwent a dramatic political metamorphosis – the impeachment of the first democratically elected president since the nation's 20-year military rule ended in 1985. In the field of communication, Brazil convened its first worldwide international congress – the biannual general meeting of the International Association for Mass Communication Research (IAMCR).

I set out to accomplish two main objectives with this book. First, by synthesizing a broad and comprehensive array of key themes in media, communication, and culture, I hope to have written a text that can be appreciated and used by scholars across a wide range of academic disciplines. I detest the practice of carving up the academy into jealously guarded intellectual provinces. Privileging certain theoretical traditions, literatures, and empirical domains according to some imagined hierarchy of intrinsic worth or correctness is a violent form of theoretical decontextualization and the worst variety of academic politics. I play to no disciplinary favorites here. Furthermore, I approach the study of communication and culture with a distinct multicultural and international tone. Many of the examples I use as an empirical foundation for developing my theoretical perspective describe settings and ways of living outside North America, the British Isles, and continental Europe. Theorists outside the northern loop, notably Néstor García Canclini of Mexico and Jesús Martín-Barbero of Colombia, are prominent contributors to the points of view that evolve in the following pages too.

Though I try to be inclusive and comprehensive, the book is also driven by a focused argument that analyzes communication processes and cultural contexts by synthesizing several of what I consider to be the most compelling streams of contemporary social and cultural theory. Along the way, distinctions often made between mass and interpersonal communication, critical and empirical research, microsocial and macrosocial domains, communication studies, cultural studies, and sociology, for example, are discarded for a more integrated approach. We study the media, communication, and culture of capitalist and communist systems, of the First World and the Third, of the rich and the poor, of the mainstream and the margins. I evaluate the role of media in a variety of world political and cultural developments extending from California to China by way of England, Brazil, and elsewhere. My overall intention is to present a well-documented and reasonable perspective that is up-to-date and accessible to a wide spectrum of readers.

To borrow a phrase from Martín-Barbero, I am interested to explore the "communicative nature of culture" (1993: 211). Communication is the conceptual meeting ground where interpersonal relations and technological innovations, political-economic incentives and sociocultural ambitions, light entertainment and serious information, local environments and global influences, form and content, substance and style intersect. I emphasize the influence of communications technology in this book because mass media continue to radically expand the nature of symbolic "co-presence" in the modern era (Thompson, 1994). We focus with a wide-angle lens on the culturally situated interplay between source, symbol, and interpreter in what Dave Morley calls the "postmodern geography of the media" (1992: 1). I argue here that mass media are not unified, monolithic forces that overwhelm isolated, dependent, passive audience members anywhere in the world. But at the same time I try to show why the ideological and cultural power of media institutions should not be underestimated either. In the end, I argue that any assessment of media influence must be understood precisely in terms of the historically situated social and cultural settings and dynamics where mediated, symbolic agendas are created and incorporated into everyday life.

In the first chapter I lay out the substantive contours of the basic subject matter taken up in the book by discussing three fundamental critical constructs: ideology, hegemony, and consciousness. I purposefully establish an overly deterministic view of ideology and hegemony in this chapter which I then challenge throughout the book. In chapter 2 I review social rules, a key element of the theoretical perspective advanced here. We examine how rules connect ideology to sources of social power and authority, including media authority. Culture and cultural power are discussed in chapter 3. This chapter highlights the complex and intriguing idea of "popular culture," and how people draw from their rich, expansive symbolic environments to creatively construct meaningful identities and lifestyles. The "active audience" is the subject of chapter 4 where, against a backdrop of the quantitative research tradition in mass communication, I present a critique and alternative to standard media uses and gratifications theory. In this chapter, I also discuss the importance of the imagination in communication theory. In chapter 5, "Meaning in Motion," I contrast the critical media/cultural imperialism perspective on world communication activity with the more optimistic and current constructivist views. The nature of symbolic interpretation is explored in this chapter, as are arguments making up debates about globalization and the role of modern media in the dynamic formation of new cultural territories. The concluding chapter then interfuses theoretical claims that accumulate in forerunning sections of the book. I rely on Anthony Giddens's structuration theory here to help shape the summary and synthesis. I apply Giddens's critique of structure to media institutions and his notion of social agency to culturally situated audience activity. In this way I further develop the book's defining statement, emphasizing (1) the dynamic, social nature of media institutions; (2) the open-ended character of symbolic representation; and (3) the culturally situated interpretative and utilitarian activities of media audience members. The book concludes with a positive but cautionary assessment of the tangle of contemporary media, communication, and culture which surrounds all of us.

1
Ideology, Consciousness, Hegemony

The development of critical communication and cultural theory in recent years has brought with it attention to ideology, consciousness, and hegemony. These important concepts are interrelated and overlapping, though each has a unique emphasis and role. The concepts appear in discussions that are made throughout this book. To introduce them, we can say that *ideology* is a system of ideas expressed in communication; *consciousness* is the essence or totality of attitudes, opinions, and sensitivities held by individuals or groups; and *hegemony* is the process through which "dominant" ideology is transmitted, consciousness is formed, and social power is exercised.

Ideology

In the most general and benign sense, ideology is organized thought – complements of values, orientations, and predispositions forming ideational perspectives expressed through technologically mediated and interpersonal communication. Ideologies may or may not be grounded in historically or empirically verifiable fact. They may be tightly or loosely organized. Some ideologies are complex and well integrated; others are fragmented. Some ideological lessons are temporary; others endure. Some meet strong resistance from audiences; others have immediate and phenomenal success. But the indeterminate character of ideology should not obscure its importance. Organized thought is never innocent. Ideologies are implicated by their origins, their institutional associations, and the purposes to which they are put, though these histories and relationships may never be entirely clear.

Ideology is a fit expression to describe the values and public agenda of nations, religious groups, political candidates and movements, business organizations, schools, labor unions, even professional sporting teams and rock bands. But the term most often refers to the relationship between information and social power in large-scale, political-economic contexts. In this sense, selected ways of thinking are advocated through a variety of channels by those in society who have political and economic power. The ongoing manipulation of public information and imagery constructs a potent *dominant ideology* which helps sustain the material and cultural interests of its creators. Fabricators of dominant ideologies become an "information elite." Their power, or dominance, stems directly from their ability to publicly articulate their preferred systems of ideas. Ideology has force, therefore, when it can be represented and communicated.

The origins of ideology as a critical concept in social theory can be traced to late eighteenth century France (Thompson, 1990). Since then, by one definition or another, ideology has been a central concern of historians, literary critics, philosophers, semioticians, rhetoricians – theorists representing virtually every niche in the humanities and social sciences. European intellectuals in particular have given the concept a sharp critical edge. British social theorists, for example – living in a blatantly class-divided society famous for its kings and queens, princes and princesses, lords and ladies – often define ideology in terms of how information is used by one socioeconomic group (the "ruling class," in Marxist terms) to dominate the rest. Raymond Williams calls ideology "the set of ideas which arises from a given set of *material* interests or, more broadly, from a definite class or group" (1976: 156; italics mine). Stuart Hall (1977) argues that ideology, not just economic authority, shapes and maintains social class divisions in the United Kingdom and other capitalist societies. John B. Thompson insists that ideology can only properly be understood as "dominant ideology" wherein symbolic forms are used by those with power to "establish and sustain relations of [asymmetrical social] domination" (1990: 58). The socioeconomic elites are able to saturate society with their preferred ideological agenda because they control the institutions that dispense symbolic forms of communication, including the mass media.

We frequently hear the term "ideology" mentioned in political-economic analyses, not only in academic arguments fashioned by critical theorists, but in journalistic accounts as well. The expressions "capitalist ideology" and "socialist ideology," for example, can be used synonymously with "capitalism" and "socialism" to refer to the fundamental theoretical principles that underlie the two political-economic-cultural systems. This linguistic interchangeability reveals both the essence and the critical nature of the concepts. Even unreflectively invoking the term "ideology" calls attention to the values and practices of capitalism and socialism as political-economic-cultural schema that are constructed and represented rather than natural and self-evident. It problematizes the systems as sets of values, perspectives, and conforming social practices. This seemingly minor shift of language can facilitate analysis and debate, and that is a main reason why the term "ideology" is a favorite of critical observers and theorists.

Ideology and the mass media

> You work your buns off all those years, going up and down the highway, riding those raggedy little airplanes and stuff like that. Then I make a TV commercial with Bo Jackson – all I say is "Bo, you don't know Diddley" – and all of a sudden I'm back on top again. (Bo Diddley, American blues singer, referring to Bo Jackson, American baseball and football superstar)

Some ideological sets are elevated and amplified by the mass media, given great legitimacy by them, and distributed persuasively, often glamorously, to large audiences. In the process, selected constellations of ideas assume ever-increasing importance, reinforcing their original meanings and extending their social impact. Bo Diddley's remarks only hint at the ability of the electronic media to effectively call attention to certain symbols, persons, and ideas. Television has the unparalleled ability to expose, dramatize, and popularize cultural bits and fragments of information. It does so in the routine transmission of entertainment programs, news, and commercials. The bits and fragments then become ideological currency in social exchange. They don't stand alone. Because authorship of television's agenda rests ultimately in the hands of society's political-economic-cultural establishment, the selected information often congeals to form ideological sets that overrepresent the interests of the powerful and underrepresent the interests of others. Television may be the most obvious conveyer of dominant ideology, but all mass media, including less recognized forms such as postage stamps, store windows, automobile bumper stickers, tee-shirts, even museums and restaurant menus, carry messages that serve the interests of some groups and not others. Consider, for instance, the ideological lessons given in these familiar American bumper stickers:

- He Who Dies with the Most Toys Wins.
- I Owe, I Owe, So Off to Work I Go.
- My Other Car is a Porsche.

Image systems

Image . . . is everything. (Tennis professional Andre Agassi in a TV commercial for a Japanese camera manufacturer)

The effective spread of dominant ideologies depends on the strategic use of *image systems*, of which there are two basic types: *ideational* and *mediational* (figure 1.1). Image systems entail articulation of layers of ideological representation and the tactical employment of modern communications technology to distribute the representations, which, when successful, encourage audience acceptance and circulation of the dominant themes.

Ideational image systems

Much like language and other communication codes, ideational image systems – which I will illustrate in more concrete detail

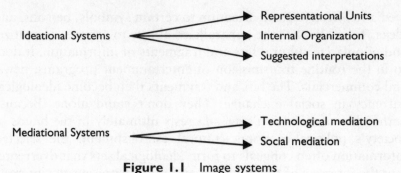

Figure 1.1 Image systems

below – are composed of units of ideational representation (morphemes), with complex internal forms of organization (syntax), that suggest and prefer particular interpretations (semantics). The mass media, especially television, "disseminate and legitimate in a pleasurable fashion, a political vocabulary that favors certain interests and groups over others . . . by giving presence to their codes" (Condit, 1989: 114). But ideology is not only made up of particular symbolic representations, each with its self-serving point of view. Ideology is also transmitted by means of a "grammar of production through which the media universalize a style of life" (Martín-Barbero, 1993: 142).

Advertising, of course, is a symbolic domain that lends itself well to ideological analysis. It's clear that what commercial advertisers sell are not just products, services, or isolated ideas. They sell multilayered, integrated ideational systems that embrace, interpret, and project interdependent images of products, idealized consumers benefiting from the products, corporations that profit from sale of the products, and, most important, the overarching political-economic-cultural structure – and the values and social activity it embraces – that presumably makes all the consumer activity possible.

Media audience members as potential consumers are encouraged to become involved with commercial products and personalities by imagining contexts – the physical scenes, emotional circumstances, and actual social situations in which they would be able to use the product. These projected *imagined situations* are grounded in an overarching *value structure* with which the consumer is already familiar. Advertising's success depends on the interpretative chemistry of plausible imagined consumptive situations interacting with familiar and accepted value structures. So, for example, a Nissan automobile commercial encourages viewers to buy one of their sleek-looking but competitively priced cars "Because rich guys shouldn't have all the fun!" These eight words sell much more than Nissans. They are used to construct an imagined situation framed by a value structure that embraces unabashed materialist competition, a commodified definition of pleasure, reinforcement of the "naturalness" of a socially stratified society, an assumption that social aggressiveness is the territory of men, and permission to use the product in order to deceive others into thinking you've got a car that reflects high socioeconomic status.

Repeated presentation of partisan ideological domains continues to define or "indicate" culture, particularly for people who are heavily exposed to media. Because media often interpret and synthesize images in accord with the assumptions of the dominant ideology, they greatly influence how people make sense of even the most basic features of their societies. This includes societies' levels of violence, racial and gender composition and roles, vocational expectations, and political alternatives (Gerbner and Gross, 1976; Gerbner, 1973). Television takes the lead. George Gerbner and Larry Gross point out that TV "is an agency of the established order and as such serves primarily to extend and maintain rather than alter, threaten, or weaken conventional conceptions, beliefs, and behaviors . . . its chief cultural function is to spread and stabilize social patterns" (1976: 175). The interrelatedness of television's main themes led these authors to call the medium's content a "message *system*." Ideologies, then, are orchestrated "maps of intelligibility," some of which are made more available than others depending on who's got the power, and mass media are the "tools of ideological representation" (Hall, 1985).

The flood of commercials capitalizing on the national mood in the United States following the Gulf War illustrates well how culturally based value structures can be used to sell products. In these commercials, sponsors positioned their products inside the emotional context of nationalism, patriotism, and militarism that swept America after Iraq surrendered – to "go with the glow," in advertising terms. Post-war accolades in political rhetoric and corporate advertising incessantly celebrated what was called America's freedom-loving spirit, its selfless determination, and its technological superiority. A fundamental objective of corporate advertising in general is to gain and maintain credibility by embedding specific messages in more abstract and encompassing ideologies in order to promote effective ideational image systems. In the case of the post Gulf War rhetoric, for example, commercial messages were reinforced almost daily by George Bush's pronouncements of America's prominent role in his imaginary "New World Order."

Nationalist rhetoric in television commercials long predates the self-congratulatory indulgences that saturated the airwaves following the Gulf War or the current exercises in Japan bashing. A common technique has been to ridicule other nations and peoples. Films, television programs, and commercials chastised Germans and Japanese for years after World War II ended. The Cold War ideological standoff in effect before *perestroika*, *glasnost*, the collapse of the Berlin Wall, and the ultimate disintegration of the Soviet Union provided a political context in which American nationalism and capitalism were exalted by blatant negative stereotyping of communist nations and peoples. The typical strategy has been to link good feelings about American culture (of which the product is a part) by encouraging the audience to laugh at the dramatized cultural (and racial) incompetencies of foreigners. Russians were frequent targets in the 1980s (see Real, 1989). The movie *Rocky IV*, for instance, depicts a robotized Russian who succumbs to a muscular American. Evil Russians are met and defeated in *Rambo* and *Red Dawn*. Soviet officers were stereotyped as clever, but bumbling, in *White Nights*. In the final scene of this film, representatives from various Third World nations stand shoulder-to-shoulder to support the United States as Soviet expatriate Mikhail Barishnikov and his American friend Gregory Hines escape the Russians. The impression given is that the United States is well liked by Third World peoples and governments – truly a twist on reality. Such nationalism is often dangerously blind. While nearly two-thirds of my 200 students approved of the American bombing of Libya the day after it happened in 1986, for example, roughly the same percentage had no idea on what continent Libya is located.

Commercial advertising not only asserts, references, and reinforces preferred ideologies, it often suggests that products and services exist to help create a better world, despite strong evidence to the contrary in many cases. Specific campaigns are designed to sell images of companies as socially responsible as much as to sell their products. This indirect technique is called institutional advertising. Warm, fuzzy, incomplete, often misleading claims – all designed to make us feel good about the sponsor and about ourselves (as Americans in this case) – are regularly made on TV to accomplish this goal. International Business Machines (IBM), for example, claims to be "helping to put information to work for people," without spelling out which people benefit, in what ways, and at whose expense. A West Coast telephone company claims that "technology will give people more time to be more human" and that we should turn responsibility for managing the technology over to them. Dow Chemical, the company that scorched Vietnam with napalm and Agent Orange, now presents dreamy *National Geographic* style visuals on its TV ads while claiming to be the company that "protects wildlife." Xerox unblinkingly says it is "documenting the world." Citicorp Bank opines that its services are necessary "because Americans want to succeed, not just survive." A TV "public service announcement" produced by the Ad Council, a federation of American advertising agencies, tells citizens that "people cause pollution, people can stop it," ignoring the fact that the most damaging environmental polluters are industrial corporations who refuse to accept the responsibility. While George Bush stoked up his 1992 re-election bid, the same Ad Council blitzed TV's airwaves with a previous Bush campaign buzz phrase – "A Thousand Points of Light" – designed once again to convince Americans that individual efforts, not structural changes, can collectively solve national problems.

Advertising reinforces the class-based structure of society by symbolically rewarding workers' contributions to the system, thereby further legitimating the system itself. The American working class is commonly saluted on American television. The humor and lifestyles of the working class are imitated in television programming, reinforcing many central beliefs and values held by American workers and their families, thereby helping to keep them amused with representations of themselves while they are encouraged to keep working and consuming. Working class spirit, a great symbol of and for America, is especially celebrated in domestic beer commercials. Blue collar work settings and leisure time activities are shown while the narrator gives the verbal reward: "For all the men and women who have served this great country, this Bud's for you" or "Buy that man a Miller." The rock band Huey Lewis and the News adapted one of their hit songs, "I'm Working for a Living," into a 1990s MTV-style beer commercial.

Explicit advertising claims are sometimes repeated so often over time that they can become part of audience members' assumptive worlds. Perhaps the best example is Bayer aspirin. The assertion for years that Bayer is the "best" aspirin has contributed, along with other marketing strategies, to a widespread perception of this brand as superior to its competitors, even though Bayer, like all other brands, contains only five-grain aspirin. Similarly, General Motors' fictitious, friendly, fair, and ever-so-competent "Mr Goodwrench" became America's generic mechanic thanks to an advertising campaign that has gone on for years. Even the body can be normalized ideologically. In an American television commercial for the cosmetic product Porcelaire (a cream that covers liver spots), a woman calls the spots on the back of her hands "beauty spots." The spokeswoman for the product quickly interjects, "Some people call those *age* spots, Peg!," correcting a (healthy) perception of the woman's skin to conform to the sponsor's objectives. And when things go wrong in marketing and advertising, sheer repetition of a positive message in the face of criticism (commercial stonewalling) is a way to overcome a damaging perception. A major lumber company indicted for irresponsibly slashing and cutting the emerald hills of America's Great Northwest, for example, referred to itself for years in TV commercials as "the tree growing company." In the unctuous wake of the Alaska oil spill, Exxon vigorously promoted an "environmentally conscious" image.

Predominant ideologies reflect the values of society's politically or economically powerful institutions and persons, regardless of the type of system in place. In capitalist countries, corporate executives greatly influence media content by sponsoring programs and advertising products. Because media content is not

Photo 1.1   The Trabant – a sometimes mobile ideological monument to communist inefficiency and drabness in the former East Germany (photo by James Lull)

sponsored directly by government or associated in the minds of most people with administrative authority, its ideological tones and trajectories are not easily recognized, a fact that helps magnify the ideological impact. Dictators in authoritarian regimes, on the other hand, restrict access to information and to communications technology in order to maintain control. Socialist nations use mass media to promote political, economic, and cultural programs that are decided upon democratically in some cases, imposed in others. In the few remaining communist nations, party officials develop explicit ideological objectives and lessons which are then sent to the people through media programming. In China, for example, television and other media are full of glaringly biased news reports, programs that salute "model workers" and "model citizens," politically correct dramas, documentaries that praise socialism and the Communist Party, and bluntly didactic editorials. Communist ideology is straightforwardly prescriptive, no apologies made. The Communist Party, after all, supposedly acts in the best interests of the people who are said to need and want ideological supervision.

Mediational image systems

Media-transmitted ideology in any political-economic-cultural context is represented partly *in* language and articulated and interpreted *through* language and other highly elaborated codes and modes – including visual forms and music – which are then further interpreted and used by people in routine social interaction. These processes are all part of the ideological effect. They comprise mediational image systems, which can be further divided into technological mediation and social mediation.

Technological mediation, of course, refers to the intervention of communications technology in social interaction. Let me again use the case of commercial advertising to illustrate the point. Billions of dollars are spent each year to find just the right mediational systems for the purposes of profit-obsessed commercial advertisers. Advertisers' strategies take advantage of the full range of mass media's persuasive potential. Selection of corporate spokespersons, visual logos, audio jingles, catchy slogans, the style and pace of commercials, special technical effects, editing conventions, product packaging, and the melding of print and electronic media campaigns, to name several central factors, all combine to generate the desired result, selling capitalism's big and bright products and the political-economic-cultural infrastructure that goes along with them.

Even mass media's presentational formats cue certain expectations and responses. When commercial advertising first appeared on television in the United States, for example, sponsors concentrated strictly on the attributes of their products. No mention was made of competitors' products, except for occasional comparisons with "Brand X." This advertising practice changed in the 1970s so that names of marketplace rivals were mentioned in commercials. When this happened, the public cried "foul!" Many people complained that it is unethical to identify the loser in a product comparison, even though this practice was never legally prohibited. The public reaction to the change reveals a crucial dimension of mass media's role as a transmitter and shaper of ideology – its power to establish and uphold widespread patterns of thought not only by repeatedly calling positive attention to particular objects of content, but by framing content in such a way that standardized presentational formats themselves connote particular ways to think. Such conventions influence not only audiences, but the creators of popular culture too. Most pop musicians, for instance, have adopted a song-writing style where the predictable formula – verse/chorus/verse/chorus/bridge/chorus – has become the norm. Global advertising and news program formats are likewise structured, imitative, and predictable.

Modern communication technologies deliver values, perspectives, and ideas to people of various cultures, social classes, and ages all over the world. Young children, of course, are particularly enthusiastic media users. Consequently, pervasive popular culture figures such as Ronald McDonald, Madonna, Tony the Tiger, Michael Jordan, and the Teenage Mutant Ninja Turtles become celebrated acquaintances and purveyors of ideology – and not just in media-saturated North America. A compilation of Walt Disney cartoons, *Mickey Mouse and Donald Duck*, became the most popular television program in the People's Republic of China by the late 1980s. Its characters challenge the sanctity and popularity of children's Chinese folk heroes such as Chi-kung, the "crazy Buddha." In order for Chi-kung to maintain an elevated position in Chinese culture today, he must appear on television. Donald Duck and his family of Disney pals have also become more familiar to children in some South American countries than the heroes of their own history and folklore (Dorfman and Mattelart, 1972). Brazilian villagers could more easily identify Michael Jackson from a photo than they could any of their own presidential candidates in 1984, although, in general, Brazilian media are far more attentive to their own cultural heroes than they are to foreign personalities (Kottak, 1990). Regardless of the source of imagery or specific content, a transformation of folkloric characters and stories from print media to television is taking place all over the world. Of course, every time a story is translated from one technology to another, the ideological representations change too. A mass medium is not a vessel which carries ideas from one place to another, but is itself a subjective, interpretative, ideological form (Martín-Barbero, 1993: 102).

Just as language and other communication codes are learned and reinforced in contexts of everyday social interaction, ideology is likewise made familiar and normal in routine social intercourse. These are the processes of *social mediation*. Mass media's ideological representations are recognized, interpreted, edited, and used in audience members' social construction of daily life. Children, for example, regularly put TV's ideologically loaded, commonly known imagery to work in their everyday communication. They often refer to TV characters, programs, and themes to explain or clarify real-world situations, enter adult conversations, and play games with their peers. But television and film provide much imagery useful to adults in their routine communications too. People commonly retell each other news stories they see on television. To call someone a "real Archie Bunker type," to say that a woman "reminds me of Roseanne," or to describe a family as "just like the Cosbys" immediately conjures up unmistakable imagery. Even Iraq's Saddam Hussein warned the Americans before the land invasion that the Gulf War was "not going to be another *Rambo* movie." He promised instead that the land war would be the "mother of all battles." When the mother of all battles failed to materialize, Americans picked up and exploited the phrase, even commercially. For months we heard about "the mother of all comebacks" on sporting fields, the "mother of all examinations" in classrooms, and "the mother of all sales" at local retail stores.

Even seemingly trivial extracts from TV commercials, news, entertainment programs, and movies take on tremendous ideological force when they are circulated socially. John B. Thompson (1990) calls this the "discursive elaboration" of ideology. Consider the following representations of media messages:

● Mexican crafts vendors walk the beach in front of Mazatlan's luxury hotels enticing North American tourists with sales pitches that feature English-language media expressions:
  "Hey, K-Mart shoppers . . ."
  "Please buy something, lady . . . go ahead, make my day!"
  "Happy hour now . . . two bracelets for the price of one."

● Popular joke following the Gulf War:
  Q: "What do you call a Scud Missile that's been intercepted by a Patriot before it falls to the ground?"

> A: "A Scud Light" (referring to Bud Light, a frequently advertised American beer).

● After the Gulf War the police department in Campbell, California labels its intensive effort to catch speeding motorists "Operation Traffic Storm."

● I explain to a checkout clerk at a supermarket near my home that I'm eating a candy bar in the late afternoon because "it's snack time." She notes what I'm eating and asks, "Isn't that supposed to be a Snickers?," referring to the candy company's advertising pitch as the snack that satisfies between meals.

● Some brand names become normative language, referring to ideas and actions that transcend the product:
"Let's have a Coke."
"I have to Xerox this report."

● The United States Defense Department urges increased military presence in Somalia in order to "Give Peace a Chance."

● Don Sutton, announcer for the Atlanta Braves baseball team, says during a broadcast that it's time for one of the team's pitchers to throw a "Visine ball." Visine is an eye-clearing product that claims it "will get the red out." Atlanta was playing the Cincinnati Reds.

● University of Kentucky basketball coach Rick Pitino claims that when his team wins games "[we] start doing the Toyota commercial" (where everyone jumps up and down).

● Drug dealers on the streets of Oakland, California market crack cocaine with names such as "Sudden Impact."

● The Beach Boys' hit song "Kokomo," in which a fictional tropical paradise is described, inspires a rush of inquiries to travel agents for tickets transporting them to the nonexistent place.

● Americans frequently hum the "do-do-do-do, do-do-do-do" music from the TV show *Twilight Zone* when something unexplainable happens.

● San Francisco Bay Area women are told to be wary of "Radar," a serial rapist said to resemble the meek character from *M.A.S.H.*

● After hearing an airline captain make his pre-takeoff remarks, a passenger says, "Wow, he sounds just like the comedian I saw on TV the other night."

These seemingly innocuous examples help illustrate how media-transmitted ideological fragments are creatively used in routine social interaction – sometimes further mediated by public institutions, including other media – and popularize selected values, ideas, slogans, and products in the process. In cases such as these, the social mediation of ideology contributes to its expansive, integrative, systemic character. All the verbalizations (and social mediations of ideology) described above "work" because of the widespread familiarity and stereotypicality of the images to which they refer, a condition directly traceable to the distributive capability of mass media technology. When people refer to media images in everyday conversations, privileged ideological themes are once again articulated and socially validated. Complex ideas are frequently reduced to catchy sound bites and advertising slogans. Furthermore, reality is framed according to prior media representations and their underlying assumptions and analogs so that mediated imagery becomes the referent with which the "real world" is often compared, an analytical inversion and ideological reification that carries enormous social implications. Not only the

Photo 1.2 Reality imitates art imitating reality. A camel rider at the pyramids outside Cairo strikes a famous pose, hoping to win tourist dollars. He announces, "Remember? Peter O'Toole . . . Lawrence of Arabia!" (photo by James Lull)

messages have an impact. When audience members repeat a phrase from TV, for example, the utility and credibility of the media technology itself is also reinforced once again.

Consciousness

Ideological image systems cannot confer meaning. The consequences of communication do not always fulfill message senders' objectives. Still, to the undeniable benefit of those who dominate the media's agenda, most people in the world's more developed societies are not only massively exposed to media, they depend on them for many things. In the United States, for instance, the typical family keeps at least one TV set turned on more than seven hours daily. Two-thirds of the American public gets all its news from TV. Consequently, Americans routinely encounter key social themes that are weighted substantially in line with sponsors' values and objectives and are fitted within the ideological contours of mainstream culture and politics. Mass media transmit highly selective images framed with ready-made viewpoints on many issues that lie outside most audience members' personal knowledge and experience. This is particularly true of global political matters. People the world over, for instance, were entirely dependent on media and government (as reported by media) for accounts of American military incursions into Lebanon, Granada, Panama, Iraq, and Somalia during the past decade alone.

Consciousness is influenced by the transmission of ideology to the extent that society's powerful institutions can infiltrate thinking and affect human action. Even when audience members flatly reject ideas expressed by the mass media, they do so only after being introduced to and, at some level, recognizing and contemplating dominant motifs in the ideological patterns mobilized before them. Of course, consciousness is not fixed; it is impermanent and malleable. It is shaped by the media, but by other information sources too. Nonetheless, consciousness reflects the inevitable inculcation of ideological themes delivered by mainstream media in ways that inspire concordant thought and social behavior. Furthermore, consciousness formation is not always self-evident. Like the fish who don't problematize the

water in which they swim, audience members don't always analyze how their everyday environments, including media symbolism, shape thinking.[1] Consciousness, thus, *must* (imperfectly and
partially) reflect the pervasive, dominant subjects and patterns of
mass-mediated ideological representation.

Sheer repetition of ideological themes can send ideas deep into
audience members' individual and collective consciousness. The
persuasive effect is always working; it doesn't occur only at the
moment of exposure. Particular expressions, and the values and
assumptions they uphold, reside like a recessive inventory of ideas
in the memory systems of people. These ideological memory
traces are evoked contextually. The dynamic relation between the
articulation of particular messages and individual consciousness
can be illustrated by how people listen and respond to popular
music. If you are asked to recite the lyrics of a popular song, for
instance, you probably cannot do so. But if a recording of the song
is played, you very well may be able to sing along perfectly.
Something quite interesting and important happens when the
music starts – a sonic context is established, acting like a cueing
system that stimulates not only recall of the words, but how they
should be sung, the melody, and, frequently, vivid sentimental
associations with people and events – interacting layers of
ideational representation.

The subconscious

Consciousness, therefore, need not imply complete or current
awareness. Furthermore, many media messages are more implicit
than explicit and are not intended to be interpreted with focused,
full awareness in the first place. An extreme example of indirect,
low-awareness ideological influence is subliminal persuasion – the
attempt to manipulate behavior by infiltrating the human subconscious. Subliminal persuasion captured the public's interest in
recent years and has been the subject of some academic studies in
the psychology of perception. Interest in subliminal persuasion
was aroused primarily by three provocative but highly speculative
books (Key, 1973; 1976; 1980). Unfortunately, the titles of these
short books (*Subliminal Seduction, Media Sexploitation, The
Clam Plate Orgy*) and the author's sensationalized treatment have
undermined serious consideration of the topic.

Photo 1.3 Let it flow. Subliminal sexual intercourse in magazine advertising (reprinted with permission)

Subliminal messages are embedded in advertising texts and in other media content. They are often designed to enhance the attractiveness of a product by appealing to subconscious, un-articulated desires. Based on motivational principles deriving from Freudian psychoanalytic theory, the persuasiveness of sub-liminal messages stems from their ability to provoke subconscious release of repressed sexual energy and by appealing to the "death wish." Subliminal messages are buried in media texts in ways that defy conscious perception. For example, subliminal film and video messages are flashed on the screen for only a fraction of a second so that viewers receive, but don't actually "see," the decontextualized messages. In recorded music, spoken messages are inserted on discs and tapes in a way that can only be detected by playing the song backwards. Print media, especially magazine advertising, contain below-the-level-of-consciousness suggestions in their photographs and graphic art.

Despite considerable popular attention given to subliminal persuasion, and the fact that it has been debated and banned by several government agencies and industry organizations, we have little scientific knowledge about it. Analyzing the effects of subliminal messages is difficult because audience members do not recognize the images. That's the point. Subliminal persuasion depends on undetected influence. In spite of problems measuring subliminal persuasion, the charlatan nature of the phenomenon itself, and the way it has been proselytized for profit, subliminal messages are not sheer folly. They are among the most subtle forms of mass media influence.

Temporal and spatial consciousness

Modern mass media, especially electronic media, organize and promote conceptions of time and space – essential features of consciousness. How technological forms affect human perceptions of and relations to time and space (also "place") has been an enduring, central question in the evolution of contemporary communications media. Harold Innis was the first writer to systematically address this issue (1950; 1951; 1952). But rather than celebrate the technological wizardry of modern media, Innis worried about their economic, political, and cultural consequences. He began by examining what *mass* communication implies – that messages become detached from their senders and from the times and contexts of production. Mediated messages are received by a great number of people at many different times in a wide range of places and circumstances. Thus, modern mass media – especially the electronic forms – make possible a unique technological conquering of time and space. However, Innis pointed out, this achievement must be qualified. In the process of spanning time

and space with unprecedented speed and efficiency, media technologies also influence the assumptions and flow of everyday life
in ways that provide tremendous advantage to those in positions
to profit from such temporal and geographic compressions and
reconfigurations. Much like advanced twentieth century transportation forms which stimulated an economic boom for urban indus-
trialists, communications media also "bind" space, according to
Innis, in ways that regulate commerce and effect social control.
The ability of newspapers, radio, and television to dramatically
reduce physical distance in human communication is at core a
form of neocolonialism. What concerned Innis, then, was that
mass-mediated time and space could be managed to economic,
political, and cultural advantage; specifically, that local, more
democratic control over these fundamental domains is lost to a
metropolitan elite whose prime motivation is to profit from a
modern type of exploitation.

Innis's writing set the stage for many more commentaries on the
crucial relationship between technological form, time and space,
and community. Most notable is the work of his fellow Canadian,
Marshall McLuhan (1962; 1964; McLuhan and Fiore, 1967).
Whereas Innis explicitly warned of the dangers he thought modern
communications technology poses to society, McLuhan was far
less critical. McLuhan claimed that electricity (and electronic
media) "abolish time and space" and what has followed in the
wake is a "global village." He claimed that each new communications medium manipulates time and space uniquely ("the medium
is the message/massage," "hot and cool media") and, consequently, that each medium in its own way greatly affects human
perception and social organization. Specifically, McLuhan argued
that print media, whose linear forms emphasize rationality, led
world cultures away from their oral, nonlinear, holistic roots. But
the current array of electronic media reconstructs nonlinearity and
"retribalizes" a new global society. While McLuhan suggested
that electronic media's refashioning of time and space has shocking implications for society, his theory of mediated communication was never coherent and was certainly not critical. He didn't
have much to say about who the chiefs of the global village are, for
instance, how much they pay their workers, or where they dump
their waste.

Fortunately, every day comes with an evening.

Photo 1.4 Media divide and capitalize the natural rhythms of time to meet the ideological preferences and production schedules of the economic elite (reprinted with permission)

An American communication theorist, Joshua Meyrowitz, tried to expand the sociological dimension of McLuhan's perspective. Meyrowitz (1985) attempts to specify what radical changes the mass media stimulate in our sense of time and space by discussing how actual social situations have been altered since the electronic media arrived full force. Social situations no longer are tied to physical locations, according to Meyrowitz, and as a result our social categories and normative forms and places of interaction are blurred. The electronic media produce a new social order, one in which distinctions between childhood and adulthood are reconstituted, gender and racial statuses and roles merge, and political authority and power relations are recast in a more democratic way. Ultimately, Meyrowitz claims that the "unique power" of television is to "break down the distinctions between here and there, live and mediated, and personal and public" (p. 308).

The shifting significance of physical space in the age of electronic media includes a substantial transformation of public ("on stage") and private ("back stage") behavior, according to Meyrowitz. This perspective – based on the work of Erving Goffman (1959; 1963; 1967; 1969) – also informs the theoretical work of Cambridge sociologists Anthony Giddens and John B. Thompson. Giddens's (1984) theory of *structuration*[2] and Thompson's (1990) theory of *mediazation* both try to account for how time and space are experienced in modern societies. But more like Innis than McLuhan or Meyrowitz, the British theorists attend to social structure as a critical factor in how time and space are perceived and used. So while Meyrowitz concludes that our world is now "relatively placeless," Thompson, for example, argues instead for a new understanding of how the mass media "extend the availability of symbolic forms in time and space" (p. 221) in order "to establish and sustain relations of domination" (p. 106).

Domestic time, space, and place

The electronic media not only prompt a rethinking and reorganization of global time and space, they also influence culturally located domestic sites – how we perceive, arrange, and use our living areas and how we interact with others who reside there. It is in domestic venues and within the contingencies of everyday routines that the introduction of new forms of communication creates situations in which people alter their worlds, sometimes radically so. It is here that time and space certainly have not been abolished, that social categories have not always merged, and that traditional lines of authority often persist, and sometimes even become stronger with the introduction of consumer technologies. Patterns of family television viewing, uses of VCR machines, and management of TV, VCR, and compact disc remote control devices, for example, all reflect gender and generational hierarchies in the world's more technologically developed countries.

The introduction of new communications equipment into the home necessarily alters the living space, how it is interpreted, and how it is used. So, for instance, when a family brings home its first TV set, regardless of where in the world it happens, domestic space and its meanings change. When my parents bought their first TV set in the early 1950s in the United States, for example, they placed it at the end of the rectangular living (or "sitting") room in the front part of the house. But from the point of view of my parents, television became an unwanted intrusion on family life within a few years. My mother insisted that we add a small room to the house especially for TV viewing – the "TV room." Placing the TV set out of the way restored the living room to its original purpose – for reading and relaxing without distraction and a setting to entertain guests.

This example reveals at least five fundamental dimensions of how a family's experience with mass media interacts with domestic space, time, and place: *reception* of television programs is *microsocial activity* that dynamically intermingles with *interpersonal relations* that are embedded within *cultural* contexts that are further affected by *social structure*. So our family's characteristic TV viewing activity, which influenced the interpretations we made of TV texts, took place under circumstances set by a parent who determined what role television should play in family life and was supported by financial circumstances sufficient to permit a range of relevant options.

Culture is a vital factor in understanding how media technologies become a part of everyday life. There are many ways to live in the global village. The meaning of home, family, and leisure time, for instance, differs greatly from culture to culture, as does routine domestic activity, including patterns in the flow of human traffic in and out of the living space, the specific functions of domestic space, and characteristic modes of mass media reception (Lull, 1988). A stark contrast to scenes in the United States is the case of China, a nation where television entered virtually every urban household during the economic boom of the early 1980s (Lull, 1991). Unfortunately, economic growth has done little to improve living conditions for Chinese families in terms of domestic space. In Shanghai, for example, families of as many as four or five members typically live in one or two small rooms. Television's impact on the family under these conditions is necessarily immense, affecting the most basic assumptions and practices of daily life. Routine domestic undertakings such as providing adequate study time and space for children and prime-time entertainment for working adults, respecting the program preferences of elderly family members, and getting enough sleep, to name some key considerations, is family work. Sorting through these priorities takes place in settings where the amount of space is extremely tight and where the number of TVs in each home (another possible way to solve conflict) is one. Under these conditions, TV viewing occurs in "public home space" compared to the relatively "private home space" characteristic of larger living areas more generally available in other countries.

India signals other contrasts. In rural India, introduction of TV into the household has restructured family members' perceptions and uses of time during the day and week in ways that have radically challenged some long-standing traditions concerning gender roles and relations, work routines, child raising, and domestic tasks. Natural time – the demarcation of temporal increments by the rising and setting of the sun – has given way to television time. Sunday has become a "TV day" in India; night-time activity now focuses on TV viewing, thereby bringing men and women together for a common form of entertainment; food and the way it is prepared have changed in the interest of preserving time for TV viewing. According to Indian researcher Neena Behl (1988), these changes in rural India's family life have democratized some aspects of domestic relations in ways not completely unlike what Meyrowitz proposes. According to Behl, TV smooths out important differences in status between male and female, old and young viewers. At the same time, however, other key features of radically stratified Indian society are reinforced in acts of television viewing. Where people sit when they watch TV, for instance, typically reflects caste differences between viewers of unrelated families and between gender-based statuses within families.

Television's alteration of time, space, and place is manifest in shifting patterns of touch, talk, sleep, food preparation and consumption, and other routine forms of communication and domestic activity all over the world. Without doubt, social assimilation of communications technology and the modifications of consciousness it stimulates have deep implications for gender relations and family life in general (e.g. Morley, 1992; 1991; 1986; Ferguson, 1989). Exactly *what* those modifications are, however, is a cultural matter. Women in Germany, for instance, often complain that television destroys marital communication, while rural Indian women say that the medium brings them closer to their husbands (Rogge and Jensen, 1988; Behl, 1988). Contrasts in television's role in the domestic life of these two nations stem in part from differences in national development. TV has simply been a part of life in Germany longer. But the dissimilarities also reflect real differences in cultural values and their corresponding social practices. Another sharp cultural contrast can be shown by comparing South American with North American and northern European families. For example, in Venezuela women are heads of the household in a majority of homes and routinely control the domestic agenda, including choice of television programs and the establishment of desired viewing environments (Barrios, 1988). Many Brazilian women, like their Venezuelan counterparts, spend their evenings watching national *telenovelas* in an atmosphere dictated by them. Family television viewing in North American, northern European, and British families, on the other hand, is far more dominated by men, at least when they are employed outside the home (Morley, 1992; 1988; 1986; Rogge and Jensen, 1988; Lindlof et al., 1988; Lull, 1990; 1988). In Japan another domestic development is taking place. Because of the tremendous amount of time Japanese men spend at work and in traffic every day, women and children gradually have assumed more and more influence over television and video viewing and other home activities.

Just as families, houses, homes, everyday activities, and conceptions of time, space, and place vary within and among nations and cultures, so too do the institutional features of television, its content, and its modes of transmission. The number of channels available for viewing, program priorities and types, program scheduling, and the availability of VCRs, for instance, all extend certain cultural values and practices, thereby influencing how people watch television (Lull, 1988).[3] But while TV clearly impacts domestic life in differing ways all over the world, audiences in those same places have influenced the institution of television too. The electronic medium doesn't just dictate expectations and regulate social activity; it also responds to cultural patterns. This has often been said of program ratings in the sense that statistical approximations of audience acceptance ultimately determine the success of a program. But it is also true of other aspects of television viewing. On the West Coast of the United States in early 1992, for instance, major network affiliate stations moved "prime-time" from 8–11 p.m. to 7–10 p.m. Aging baby boom generation parents, it seems, are going to bed earlier than before, causing a slip in network ratings for the last hour's programs. Network television schedules were moved up in order to keep viewers for the high-revenue-producing final hour of prime-time and the local newscasts which follow.

No individual person, social group, or institution dispenses ideology as attractively and continuously as the mass media. Despite this awesome power, people are not unthinkingly stimulated by mediated representations of political positions, product advertising, or other ideological domains. Ideational and mediational image systems ultimately are not perfect unities and people are not imitating dupes in any political-economic-cultural environment. Individual and collective consciousness is in no case simply a product of ideological representation or technological influence. One way to interpret the complex dialectic between institutionally sponsored, technologically mediated ideas and culturally situated, intentional social action is the third basic concept addressed in this chapter – hegemony.

Hegemony

Hegemony is the power or dominance that one social group holds over others. This can refer to the "asymmetrical interdependence" of political-economic-cultural relations between and among nation-states (Straubhaar, 1991) or differences between and among social classes within a nation. Hegemony is "dominance and subordination in the field of relations structured by power" (Hall, 1985). But hegemony is more than social power itself; it is a method for gaining and maintaining power.

Classical Marxist theory, of course, stresses economic position as the strongest predictor of social differences. Today, more than a century after Karl Marx and Friedrich Engels wrote their treatises about capitalist exploitation of the working class, economic disparities still underlie and help reproduce social inequalities in industrialized societies. In that important, basic sense, Marxism and Marxist critical theory, which have been so badly maligned in the rhetoric surrounding the recent political transformation of communist nations, remain fundamentally on target. Technological developments in the twentieth century, however, have made the manner of social domination much more complex than before. Social class differences in today's world are not determined solely or directly by economic factors. Ideological influence is crucial now in the exercise of social power.

The Italian intellectual Antonio Gramsci – to whom the term hegemony is attributed – broadened materialist Marxist theory into the realm of ideology. Persecuted by his country's then fascist government (and writing from prison), Gramsci emphasized society's "super structure," its ideology-producing institutions, in struggles over meaning and power (1971; 1973; 1978; see also Boggs, 1976; Sassoon, 1980; and Simon, 1982). A shift in critical theory thus was made away from a preoccupation with capitalist society's "base" (its economic foundation) and towards its dominant dispensaries of ideas. Attention was given to the structuring of authority and dependence in symbolic environments that correspond to, but are not the same as, economically determined class-based structures and processes of industrial production. Such a theoretical turn seems a natural and necessary development in an era when communications technology is such a pervasive and potent ideological medium. According to Gramsci's theory of ideological hegemony, mass media are tools that ruling elites use to "perpetuate their power, wealth, and status [by popularizing] their own philosophy, culture and morality" (Boggs, 1976: 39). The mass media uniquely "introduce elements into individual consciousness that would not otherwise appear there, but will not be rejected by consciousness because they are so commonly shared in the cultural community" (Nordenstreng, 1977: 276). Owners and managers of media industries can produce and reproduce the content, inflections, and tones of ideas favorable to them far more easily than other social groups because they manage key socializing institutions, thereby guaranteeing that their points of view are constantly and attractively cast into the public arena.

Mass-mediated ideologies are corroborated and strengthened by an interlocking system of efficacious information-distributing agencies and taken-for-granted social practices that permeate every aspect of social and cultural reality. Messages supportive of the status quo emanating from schools, businesses, political organizations, trade unions, religious groups, the military, and the mass media all dovetail together ideologically. This inter-articulating, mutually reinforcing process of ideological influence is the essence of hegemony. Society's most entrenched and powerful institutions – which all depend in one way or another on the same sources for economic support – fundamentally agree with each other ideologically.

Hegemony is not a *direct* stimulation of thought or action, but, according to Stuart Hall, is a "framing [of] all competing definitions of reality within [the dominant class's] range, bringing all alternatives within their horizons of thought. [The dominant class] sets the limits – mental and structural – within which subordinate classes 'live' and make sense of their subordination in such a way as to sustain the dominance of those ruling over them" (1977: 333). British social theorist Philip Elliott suggested similarly that the most potent effect of mass media is how they subtly influence their audiences to perceive social roles and routine personal activities. The controlling economic forces in society use the mass media to provide a "rhetoric [through] which these [concepts] are labeled, evaluated, and explained" (1974: 262). Television commercials, for example, encourage audiences to think of themselves as "markets rather than as a public, as consumers rather than citizens" (Gitlin, 1979: 255).

But hegemony does not mature strictly from ideological articulation. Dominant ideological streams must be subsequently reproduced in the activities of our most basic social units – families, workplace networks, and friendship groups in the many sites and undertakings of everyday life. Gramsci's theory of hegemony, therefore, connects ideological representation to culture. Hegemony requires that ideological assertions become self-evident cultural assumptions. Its effectiveness depends on subordinated peoples accepting the dominant ideology as "normal reality or common sense . . . in active forms of experience and consciousness" (Williams, 1976: 145). Because information and entertainment technology is so thoroughly integrated into the everyday realities of modern societies, mass media's social influence is not always recognized, discussed, or criticized, particularly in societies where the overall standard of living is relatively high. Hegemony, therefore, can easily go undetected (Bausinger, 1984).

Hegemony implies a willing agreement by people to be governed by principles, rules, and laws they believe operate in their best interests, even though in actual practice they may not. Social consent can be a more effective means of control than coercion or force. Again, Raymond Williams: "The idea of hegemony, in its wide sense, is . . . especially important in societies [where] electoral politics and public opinion are significant factors, and in which social practice is seen to depend on consent to certain dominant ideas which in fact express the needs of a dominant class" (1976: 145). Thus, in the words of Colombian communication theorist Jesús Martín-Barbero, "one class exercises hegemony to the extent that the dominating class has interests which the subaltern classes recognize as being in some degree their interests too" (1993: 74).

Relationships between and among the major information-diffusing, socializing agencies of a society and the interacting, cumulative, socially accepted ideological orientations they create and sustain is the essence of hegemony. The American television industry, for instance, connects with other large industries, especially advertising companies but also national and multinational corporations that produce, distribute, and market a wide range of commodities. So, for example, commercial TV networks no longer buy original children's television shows. Network executives only want new program ideas associated with successful retail products already marketed to children. By late 1990 more than 20 toy-based TV shows appeared on American commercial TV weekly. Television also has the ability to absorb other major social institutions – organized religion, for instance – and turn them into popular culture. The TV industry also connects with government institutions, including especially the federal agencies that are supposed to regulate telecommunications. The development of

American commercial broadcasting is a vivid example of how capitalist economic forces assert their power. Evacuation of the legislatively mandated public service ideal could only have taken place because the Federal Communications Commission stepped aside while commercial interests amassed power and expanded their influence. Symptomatic of the problem is the fact that government regulators typically are recruited from, and return to, the very industries they are supposed to monitor.

Transmedia and transgenre integrations with mutually reinforcing ideological consequences are also commonplace. Popular radio and video songs, for example, can also be commercials. Genesis' "Tonight, Tonight, Tonight" and Steve Winwood's "Do You Know What the Night Can Do?" have the same melodies as, and similar lyrics to, the Michelob beer commercials these artists also sing. America's first prime-time, network TV, Spanish-language commercial featured Puerto Rican pop singer Chayanne reworking the lyrics of his hit song on the Latin charts, "Éste Ritmo se Baila Así," into a Pepsi-Cola endorsement. A paid-for Pepsi logo pops up in a Nintendo video game. Video games, computer games, toys, and board games pick up media/military sloganeering such as "A Line in the Sand" and "Gulf Strike." The highly rated video game Street Fighter II inspires production of a movie by the same name. Sylvester Stallone's and Wesley Snipes' *Demolition Man* becomes a movie-length commercial for the Mexican fast-food chain, Taco Bell. Sports stadiums are named after corporations and commercial products – Great Western [bank] Forum in Los Angeles, Arco [gasoline] Arena in Sacramento, Busch [beer] Stadium in St Louis, United [airlines] Center in Chicago (where United Airlines tickets are dispensed by machine in the lobby). Bill Cosby parlays his widespread recognition as a TV character into best-selling pop books on fatherhood. Commercial logos become products themselves and are reproduced on tee-shirts, posters, beach towels, and other informal media. The rhetoric of TV commercials and programs is recycled in the lyrics of rap music and in the routines of stand-up comedians performing live and on television. A romantic encounter depicted in a TV commercial for coffee (Taster's Choice in the USA; Nescafé Gold Blend in the UK) is turned into a commercial video and novel. Cable television ushers in an era of program-length commercials. There are films made for television, magazines published about television, and television news magazines. The most well-known national newspaper in the United States, *USA Today*, is sold nationwide in vending boxes that resemble TV sets. Television commercials appear on Channel One, an educational news channel shown to students in American elementary school classrooms. Logos that advertise only national gasoline, food, and motel chains appear on government highway signs, advising travelers of their availability at upcoming freeway exits. Expensive public relations campaigns of major corporations distribute "informational" supplementary textbooks to elementary and secondary school systems. Major business organizations send digests of their annual reports and other promotional materials to college instructors, hoping this biased information will be incorporated into teaching and research. Similar materials are sent to political and religious leaders so they will pass the information along to their constituencies and congregations.

In the United States, advocacy of alternative political ideologies, parties, and candidates, or suggestions of viable consumer alternatives to the commercial frenzy stimulated and reinforced by advertising and other marketing techniques, are rarely seen on the popular media. Radical ideas typically appear only on underfinanced, noncommercial radio and TV stations and in low-budget print media. These media have tiny public followings compared to commercial television and video outlets, metropolitan daily newspapers, and national magazines. When genuinely divergent views appear on mainstream media, the information is frequently shown in an unfavorable light or is modified and coopted to surrender to the embrace of mainstream thought. Thus, presidential candidate Jesse Jackson modified his unconventional political platform in 1984 to fit into the wholly unthreatening ideology of the Democratic Party; the long-haired look of "anti-establishment" young men in the 1960s became a popular hairstyle of middle-aged businessmen two decades later; roughly textured punk rock turned quickly into "new wave" dance music and was used to market radical chic department-store fashion a decade later; the anti-fashion grunge look of the 1990s is packaged for sale by fashion designer Perry Ellis; the Smothers Brothers comedy team, who championed the cause of socialist folk singer

Pete Seeger in the 1960s, do TV commercials for the Colonel Sanders' Kentucky Fried Chicken franchise; political radical Jerry Rubin is celebrated by the media as a successful stockbroker; the Jefferson Starship rock band (formerly the Jefferson Airplane, known for "We Gotta Have a Revolution" and "Up Against the Wall, Motherfucker") sells the rights to a hit song ("We Built This City") to International Telephone and Telegraph (ITT) where the song becomes an anthem for a TV commercial campaign titled "We Built This Business;" and so on. The mass media help create an impression that even society's roughest edges ultimately must conform to the conventional contours of dominant ideologies.

Hegemony has been central to the management of ideology in communist nations too, though it develops differently. Central ideological planning and the creation of propaganda to advise "the people" represent the same intention – to protect the interests of ruling elites. Sloganeering is a common strategy. In China, for example, "Respect the Four Cardinal Principles of Socialism" and "Unite Behind the Material and Spiritual Modernization" are all too familiar to the people. Educational institutions in China are required not only to teach Communist Party ideology, but to discourage any questioning of the official agenda. Journalists are supposed to find facts to support official positions rather than try to more objectively report news events.

The collapse of political authority in Eastern and Central Europe and the former Soviet Union was a breakdown in communist ideological hegemony. Conflict between culture producers and young audiences in East Germany and Hungary is typical of what happened in the Soviet bloc (Wicke, 1992; Szemere, 1985). Young rock musicians and their enthusiastic audiences led a cultural and political struggle against the repressive institutions and the ideology behind them. Trying to contain and control rebellious youth, the former communist governments attempted in sinister ways to defuse the politically charged musical and cultural activity of youth by incorporating and sponsoring them. Young people and other dissenters saw through the strategy, however, challenged the hegemony, and stimulated policy changes that later contributed to the dramatic downfall of the European communist governments. In China, the extraordinary student and worker uprising in 1989 is but the most visible sign of widespread resistance among that

country's disaffected urban population.[4] Recent popular revolu-
tions in communist countries developed from widespread discon-
tent with an interacting spectrum of economic, political, and
cultural conditions. Ironically, the workers' uprising that Marx
and Engels theorized would take place in repressive, class-based
capitalist economies developed instead in communist nations
which had proven in many respects to be even more repressive.

Hegemony as an incomplete process

Two of our leading critical theorists, Raymond Williams and
Stuart Hall, remind us that hegemony in any political context is
indeed fragile. It requires renewal and modification through the
assertion and reassertion of power. Hall suggests that "it is crucial
to the concept that hegemony is not a 'given' and permanent state
of affairs, but it has to be actively won and secured; it can also be
lost" (1977: 333). Ideological work is the winning and securing
of hegemony over time. Williams (1975) puts it another way.
He notes that not only must "technological determinism" (a
McLuhanesque perspective) be rejected as a satisfactory explanation for media effects, but so too "determined technology."
According to Williams, "Determination is a real social process but
[it] never [acts] as a wholly controlling, wholly predicting set of
causes . . . we have to think of determination not as a single
force . . . but as a process in which real determining factors – the
distribution of power or of capital, social and physical inheritance,
relations of scale and size between groups – set limits and exert
pressures, but neither wholly control nor wholly predict the outcome of complex activity" (p. 130). Ideology is composed of
"texts that are not closed" according to Hall, who also notes that
ideological "counter-tendencies" regularly appear in the seams
and cracks of dominant forms (Hall, 1985). Mediated communications ranging from popular television shows to rap and rock
music, even graffiti scrawled over surfaces of public spaces, all
inscribe messages that challenge central political positions and
cultural assumptions.

Counter-hegemonic tendencies do not inhere solely in texts.
They are formulated in processes of communication – in the
interpretations, social circulation, and uses of media content. As

with the American soldiers' use of military gas masks as inhaling devices to heighten the effect of marijuana smoke, or the homeless's transformation of supermarket shopping carts into personal storage vehicles, ideological resistance and appropriation frequently involve reinventing institutional messages for purposes that differ greatly from their creators' intentions. Expressions of the dominant ideology are sometimes reformulated to assert alternative, often completely resistant or contradictory messages. This is frequently accomplished in humorous, sarcastic ways. Consider these examples:

- Printed above the inside door of every subway car in London is the following instruction:

  Do not obstruct the door. It causes delay and can be dangerous.

  I watch two London punks completely reformulate the institutional message, inviting a thoroughly unintended and opposite public response by simply blotting out some of the words:

  obstruct the door.   cause delay   be dangerous.

- A well-known message about parenting and psychology that appears on many automobile bumper stickers in the United States is "Have You Hugged Your Kid Today?" That's been reframed into another bumper sticker: "Have You Slugged Your Kid Today?"
- Many large American companies try to keep their truck drivers in line by putting signs on the back of company vehicles that ask something like "Am I Driving Safely? If Not, Call 1-800-BIG CORP." Resisting this form of control, an alternative bumper sticker surfaces on the back of vehicles: "If You Don't Like the Way I'm Driving, Call 1-800- EAT SHIT."
- The drive-in fast-food chain "In and Out Burger" bumper sticker becomes "In and Out urge."
- The snow ski lodge "Ski Bear" becomes "Ski Bare."
- Nancy Reagan's "Just Say No To Drugs" resurfaces as "Just Say No to Drug Tests."
- Barney, the harmless, ever-so-lovable purple dinosaur who is the star of the highest-rated public TV show for children in the United States, *Barney and Friends*, becomes a fierce object of hate. A Barney lookalike was viciously attacked in a Texas shopping mall, and an "I Hate Barney Secret Society" has formed, turning

Barney's "I Love You, You Love Me" theme song into "I Hate You, You Hate Me, Let's Go Out and Kill Barney!"

● The organization Mothers Against Drunk Drivers (MADD) finds opposition from Drunks Against Mad Mothers (DAMM). Witty newspaper columnist Joe Bob Briggs further advises readers: "Mad Mothers got liquor banned on college campuses this year, even though thousands of innocent drunks continue to be killed each year by sober mothers turnin' right out of the left hand lane!"

Resistance to hegemony, of course, does not always take the form of such blatantly opposing, often humorous, ideological conversions. And hegemony is never trivial. The examples above do not always speak to the serious, overarching political and economic control that concerns Gramsci, Williams, Hall, Giddens, and Thompson. But they do reveal the independence of thought, creativity, determination, and resistance that hegemony cannot destroy. Furthermore, resistance to hegemony is not initiated solely by media consumers. Texts themselves are implicated. Ideology can never be stated purely and simply. Ways of thinking are

Photo 1.5 Counter-hegemonic resistance. Political graffiti is used to override a racist commercial message of the dominant culture (photo by James Lull)

always reflexive and embedded in a complex, sometimes contra-dictory, ideological regress. The widespread, multi-institutional "Just Say No To Drugs" campaign, for instance, is cast within a long-standing, media-perpetuated endorsement of (prescriptive) drugs as solutions to an entire range of problems. Illegal drugs have also been celebrated for years in all forms of art, especially music. A national "safe sex" campaign has not been able to stem the tide of risky sexual behavior. Part of the reason is that the mass media, even with Magic Johnson's still-smiling face on camera, have never stopped gushing positive images of devil-may-care sex. The federal government finally admitted that sexual activity among teenage girls in America increased sharply in the 1980s, despite all the anti-AIDS hype. AIDS researchers at the University of California in San Francisco, working on worldwide information campaigns about the disease, finally admitted in the early 1990s that the only real hope for slowing down the spread of the HIV virus is development of an effective vaccine.

Well-coordinated, massively sponsored commercial campaigns can never guarantee success. American business has its tragic commercial failures, perhaps still best represented by the miserable failure of the infamous Ford Edsel, a grandly promoted car in the 1950s, to entice consumers. Furthermore, counter-tendencies develop *within* ideology-transmitting institutions themselves. Horace Newcomb and Paul Hirsch, for example, point out that contrary to any theory of capitalist ideological unity, television actually emphasizes "contradiction and conflict rather than coher-ence" in its programs (1987: 62). This electronic amplification of contradiction exists in communist countries too. The Chinese government has been unable to control the ideological agenda of its own mass media, despite surface appearances of effective cen-sorship (Lull, 1991). In South Africa, racial conflict was not dis-cussed in government TV shows, but regularly appeared as themes of foreign programs, especially American films, scheduled for tele-vision airplay by progressive thinkers in the nation's television system. Priorities cultivated within the economic system can abuse its own ideology too. The late Philippines dictator Ferdinand Marcos, for instance, was cut off mid-sentence in his blatant advocacy of unbridled capitalism on a *Night Line* interview with Ted Koppel when the network satellite contract expired and the picture from Manila went black. Audience interpretations and uses of media imagery also eat away at hegemony. Hegemony fails when dominant ideology is weaker than social resistance. Gay subcultures, feminist organizations, environmental groups, radical political parties, music-based formations such as punks, B-boys, Rastafarians, and metal heads all use media and their social networks to endorse counter-hegemonic values and lifestyles. Indeed, we have only just begun to examine the complex relationship between ideological representation and social action.

Summary

In this chapter I defined the key concepts of ideology, consciousness, and hegemony and discussed how they interrelate within processes of modern human communication. I gave special attention to dominant ideology and how ideological representation can be used to exercise social power. I proposed that ideational and mediational (both technological and social) image systems underlie ideology's persuasive influence. Individual and collective consciousness to some degree reflects patterns of ideological representation, cultivating perceptions of cultural themes and conceptions of time, space, and place. Institutional interdependencies and textual congruities produce, sustain, and expand dominant modes of thought and action in processes of ideological hegemony.

In reality, however, dominant ideologies are not unified codes. Media imagery contains variety and contradiction. Furthermore, the effects of ideological representation and technological mediations cannot easily be predicted. There is no uniform social response to the perspectives put forward by the mass media and other public dispensaries of information. While dominant ideologies are cultivated hegemonically and contribute to the formation of mainstream consciousness, human beings – as individuals, audience members, family members, workers, students, and members of a multitude of formal and informal social groups – interpret and use mass media (both their content and form) in ways that surely don't always coincide with the message senders' intentions. Furthermore, nonmainstream (sometimes radical) ideologies are spread via alternative (underground, secondary, deviant) media and help develop alternative (sometimes subversive) social patterns too. Ideology, media, and social activity, therefore, all embrace areas of conformity and contestation. We will analyze how these complex forces are organized, related to social power, and integrated into the culturally situated places and times of our everyday lives throughout the rest of this book.

2

Social Rules and Power

Just as we have maps in our heads for navigating our way through physical space, so too do we have mental guidelines for negotiating social territories. We undertake these journeys successfully most of the time because the worlds we encounter are relatively coherent and consistent and because we are skilled at recognizing social prescriptions and patterns, responding and adapting, even transforming them frequently without thinking much about what we are doing. How is this immense coordination of social activity made possible and what are its consequences? What roles do mass media play in the process? In this chapter we will try to answer these questions by exploring the concept of *rule* and its complex relation to issues raised in the previous chapter, especially the exercise of social *power*. Specifically, I will describe what rules are and how they link ideology with various forms of authority in symbolic representation and social practice.

Rule

Rule is a term familiar to most everyone. Rules often tell us what is required, what is forbidden, or how to do something. Every bureaucrat and government official in the USA has convened under Roberts' Rules of Order. Judges impose rules of the court and teachers have rules for the classroom. Rules regulate sporting games, etiquette, driving, and countless other situations where safety, fairness, correctness, or efficiency are desired. Books have been written to explain the rules for playing golf, for becoming a successful businesswoman, for constructing nuclear power plants, and for maximizing sexual potential. There are rules for rulers and for radicals, for kings and for housewives, for the mind and for chaos. There are rules for breaking the rules and more rules for dealing with rule breakers. And while many rules are codified and articulated through official channels, the vast majority of rules are rarely, if ever, formalized. Informal rules of social conduct make up the cultural base of societies everywhere. It is no wonder, then, that rule has emerged as a central theoretical concept in academic disciplines such as anthropology, linguistics, sociology, political science, and communication. But rules are certainly not just the domain of academic theorists. Popular epistemologies – how people from all walks of life come to know their worlds and engage the contours and contingencies of everyday routines – are also based in rules. But what exactly are rules?

Following the seminal writing of the eighteenth-century German philosopher Immanuel Kant, rules are, first of all, *constitutive* expressions. They outline possible courses of human thought and action by pre-interpreting the world for us – by constituting, and thereby explaining and prescribing, social reality in certain ways. Rule is a structuring principle through which we make sense of the symbolic representations and social patterns we routinely encounter. Rules (often implicitly) tell us what exists, in what measure, and in what relation. Second, rules *regulate* social behavior inside the structured reality by specifically guiding and sanctioning human activity in particular ways. Rules impose systems of order on all forms of social interaction (Collett, 1977; Giddens, 1984; Cushman and Whiting, 1972). They tell us how to do things. So, rules accomplish two basic tasks: they direct social thought and action by asserting in a complex way *what* is normal, acceptable, or preferred, and they specify *how* social interaction is to be carried out. In this way, rules lead to interpersonally coordinated understandings that underlie and promote patterned social activity. They reflect cultural values and ideologies that have become identified, legitimized, concretized, and extended through time and space by specific histories of social action. Rules are the perceived ideational matrices of social organization – ephemeral referents that are kept in mind by social actors as they imagine the future in part by referring to the past. Just as the retina of the eye produces a structured image of an object even after it physically disappears from view, thereby giving continuity to sight, rules assert frameworks for ideological continuity that likewise persist in time and space. They structure the cognitive schemata and emotional inclinations people routinely use to organize, create, and find pleasure in even the most subtle circumstances of their everyday lives. It is the very embeddedness of rules in normative social practice, especially the structuring capability of the implicit, taken-for-granted rules pervading the most mundane recesses of everyday life, that gives them such great influence.

The constitutive and regulative qualities of rules generate a "shared understanding of how people ought to behave" in order to produce "consistency, regularity, and continuity" in their social worlds (Edgerton, 1985: 24, 8). When rules are widely known, and where compliance is a shared value, rules "specify 'correct' or 'appropriate' [social] procedures and the attendant community evaluates the performance" (Collett, 1977: 8). For rules to effec-tively prescribe social attitudes and activities, they must be "followable" (Shimanoff, 1980). The power of rules springs in large measure from the fact that people choose courses of action, that they are not coerced. Social actors elect to follow, ignore, break, or modify rules. Even international political relations – negotiations that affect the very future of the planet – are played by "rules of the game" (Kratochwil, 1989). The Cold War era policy of nuclear deterrence was an especially dramatic example of this.

Rules in society

Rules help construct and perpetuate the fundamental themes, trajectories, and tones of our social worlds. They do so frequently in very subtle and complex ways. *We are socialized not simply by ideas, but by the way ideas are structured, related to authority, and pertinent to our needs and interests.* By complying with rules, we forge patterns of "daily life [that are] known in common with others and with others taken for granted" (Garfinkel, 1967: 35). This very taken-for-grantedness implies a profound, often subconscious, acceptance of the terms of social rules. All communication experiences develop against a field of "background expectancies [whereby] persons . . . hold each other to agreements whose terms they never actually stipulate" (p. 73). These tacit agreements regulate the most basic, pragmatic aspects of social interaction – the volume and rhythm of interpersonal speech, for instance. Practical consciousness at core "consists of knowing the rules and the tactics whereby daily social life is constituted and reconstituted" (Giddens, 1984: 90). The relative predictability of personal habits and routines based in rule-governed social patterns helps people feel secure emotionally (Giddens, 1984; 1990; 1991).

Harold Garfinkel demonstrated the intimate relationship between and among assumptive worlds, routinization, and social order with a series of "norm breaking experiments" that his students undertook at the University of California, Los Angeles (Garfinkel, 1967). By purposefully destroying "background expectancies" and routines, Garfinkel's students instigated social chaos. A simple example is this: when the students were asked by their friends in routine interaction "How are you doing?," they were instructed by Garfinkel to ignore the social convention (which would be to say something like "Fine, thanks, how are you?" regardless of how one feels and not necessarily with any true interest in knowing how the other feels). Instead of giving the expected response, the students responded with a series of clarifying questions, taking the inquiry "How are you doing?" seriously. One response might be: "What do you mean, 'How am I doing?' Physically? Mentally? Spiritually?" Disturbed by this dismantling of a taken-for-granted way of communicating, the person who asked "How are you doing?" usually became extremely frustrated and sometimes quite angry. What this example and similar exercises reveal is the deep structure of routine social behavior and the commitment we have to act normatively in carrying out even the most seemingly unimportant everyday activities.

Garfinkel coined the term *ethnomethodology*. This expression refers not to a research strategy (for which it is frequently mistaken), but to the "methods" people use to make sense of their worlds and construct their everyday lives. These methods are central not only to practical construction of the worlds we live in, as the norm breaking experiments show, but to how we view and rationalize that world. Social actors normalize their experiences by interpreting the world in terms of their structured background expectancies. To illustrate this, let me provide an example from my own teaching experience. I asked my students at the University of Wisconsin years ago to design and carry out a naturalistic norm breaking experiment *à la* Garfinkel. Responding to the assignment, two thoroughly heterosexual Midwestern males developed a team project. One of them went into a jewelry store and stood at the counter admiring the rings. The other student, a man of about 21 years, then entered the store. The two didn't acknowledge each other's presence. They were, apparently, strangers. The second student then asked the clerk for some help picking out wedding rings. When the clerk showed some matched sets, the young man explained, in a completely unaffected tone of voice, that he wanted matching rings for *men*! The clerk, quite taken aback, shuffled some boxes around and explained that he was sure something could be worked out. The student-shopper then looked at several possible purchases, maintaining a completely straight demeanor, before thanking the employee, saying he wanted to think about it for a while, and walking out. The first student, still in the store, then moved to a spot where he could overhear the clerk re-create the scene that had just taken place. As the clerk told the story to a fellow employee, the clerk adopted a dripping, completely misleading feminine vocal affectation as he played the role of the apparently gay shopper. The assumptive world disrupted by the shopper had been reconstructed by the clerk. His re-creation of the unsettling scene restored order by reasserting what he perceived as normal gay speech. He could then recoup the reasonableness of what had happened.

Humor is often used by people in attempts to normalize shattered background expectancies. I watched a tourist in Mexico once try to bargain with a street vendor by offering to pay "only" 300,000 pesos for a beach towel. When his wife pointed out to him that this amount of Mexican currency at that time was worth more than a hundred dollars, the embarrassed man retracted his offer and joked, "Boy, we'd have to frame the sucker at that price!" Underlying such attempts at humor are strategies used to make social interaction normal when it goes wrong.

Most of us willingly abide by social rules most of the time, especially the countless unspoken rules. This is how societies function and avoid disorder. Failure to abide by social rules is even sometimes considered pathological, "dysfunctional behavior." But we must be very careful here. Evaluations of functionality are necessarily biased. What is considered functional or dysfunctional, normal or deviant, stabilizing or disruptive is always an interpretation made by individuals or groups in accord with their own world views and motivations. As Robert Merton (1957) pointed out years ago, conventional social practices frequently function to the benefit more of powerful subgroups than of marginalized groups or even of society as a whole. To understand rules, their creators, articulators, and enforcers, as well as their consequences, we must always ask: for *whom* do rules function?

Implicit rules are especially subject to strategic interpretation and manipulation. Precisely because they are not formally outlined or limited, and therefore offer little room for appeal or grievance when violated, they can be used to oppress and control. I attended a faculty meeting once where a graduate teaching assistant was actually terminated from his job not for the official reason, budgetary problems, but because he routinely used an informally unapproved form of transportation, a skateboard, to travel across campus on his way to the classes he was teaching. It became clear during the discussion of his work that several faculty members (not me, mind you, I have my own skateboard) had simply been insulted by his breaking of an unspoken rule of professional conduct. Normative rules are embedded so deeply in routine social interaction that they often are not brought to conscious awareness until the tacit requirements they embrace are disobeyed.

Although rules are pervasive and influential, they are by no means uniform, permanent, or universal. The basic distinction I have made between explicit and implicit rules reveals how widely they can differ. Some rules are clear while others are ambiguous. Some are specific to certain situations while others apply more generally. Rules vary in their degree of articulated importance and interpreted seriousness. They are hierarchical. Some rules can be broken by some people, but not by others. Some rules remain relatively unchallenged while others are regularly contested. Some rules contradict other rules.

Above all else, rules are malleable. They can be manipulated to serve the purposes of issuing authorities, but they can also be creatively used even by those with little official authority. People do not engage rules uniformly. They often interpret, use, and transform rules in ways that benefit them. Like the symbolic spheres of TV programs, music, film, literature, and all the rest of popular culture, rules themselves are resources that can be appropriated in the construction of everyday life. As John B. Thompson puts it:

> in drawing upon rules and conventions of various kinds, individuals . . . extend and adapt these schemata and rules. Every application involves responding to circumstances which are, in some respects, new. Hence the application of rules and schemata cannot be understood as a mechanical operation, as if actions were rigidly determined by them. Rather, the application of rules and schemata is a creative process which often involves some degree of selection and judgement, and in which the rules and schemata may be modified and transformed in the very process of application. (1990: 148–9)

A key concept related to rule flexibility is *exception*. When can a rule be ignored, broken, or modified? How is it done? The American anthropologist Robert Edgerton argues that rules are routinely broken depending on a variety of contextual factors including temporary conditions (e.g. when a person is ill or intoxicated); the statuses of the people involved (e.g. rich versus poor, men versus women, adults versus children); special occasions (e.g. parties, holidays, rituals); and settings (e.g. public versus private space). But rule breaking isn't always sanctioned by context. Rules are also broken for a wide variety of political, cultural, social, and personal reasons. Disruptive rule breaking can even be heroic. Although rule breakers are generally despised and often punished by institutional authorities, they are frequently celebrated culturally, especially by the mass media. Many of the most well-known movie stars (for example, James Dean, Marilyn Monroe, Marlon Brando, Eddie Murphy) and pop music celebrities (the Beatles,

Prince, and Madonna, for instance) have won huge audiences in part because they have routinely broken social and artistic rules. A young American performance artist, Dennis Leary, observes that he now gets paid big money for doing exactly the same things that got him into serious trouble at home and school. By reframing reality in novel ways, artists of all kinds can provoke feelings and stimulate unique insights. The shock of a creatively broken rule, a radical divergence from what is expected, draws attention and stimulates curiosity. Paul Bouissac (1976), for example, argues that rule breaking is at the heart of why people enjoy the circus. According to Bouissac, the circus is amusing precisely because expected patterns of everyday life are shattered into bits, then creatively reconstructed to form a new, perverse reality. At the circus a horse can make a fool of his trainer. A tiger can ride the back of an elephant. The elephant can use a telephone or sit at a dinner table.

One of the world's most famous rule-breaking contexts is Brazil's annual *Carnaval* celebration, which has been insightfully analyzed by the Brazilian anthropologist, Roberto DaMatta (1991). For four days immediately preceding the Christian celebration of Lent, the usual formal and informal rules of social behavior are broken with abandon. Normal social and sexual limits give way to an unspoken rule of freedom and egalitarianism which leads to temporary displays of "social inversion." Brazil's characteristic social positions and roles are reversed, particularly during the symbolic highlight of *Carnaval*, the parade of the *escolas da samba* (samba schools): men can become women, the poor don the garb of the rich, and the rich applaud the poor *favela* (shantytown) dwellers as they rise up temporarily to symbolically control Brazilian culture during this radical, but clearly demarcated, temporal context.[1] Rules, then, can be creatively interpreted and put to use, sometimes even in direct opposition to their originators' intentions or their common meanings.

Official rules often clash with rules-in-use. In Brazil (and Latin America generally), for instance, traffic lights and vehicle lane markers do not function as legally enforced requirements for proper driving. They are interpreted more as suggestions. In Rio, motorists routinely drive through red lights without thinking about stopping unless, of course, another car enters the intersection from the left or right. When a major street crosses a lesser street, the driver on the major street assumes the right of way, even when the signal in his or her direction is red. A driver entering from the lesser street must honk the horn or flash the headlights when approaching the crossway to warn oncoming drivers that he or she intends to enter the intersection, thereby invoking the official rule pertaining to "right of way." This example of driving in Brazil shows that rules are almost always negotiated. The negotiations themselves are rule based and culturally differentiated. A student in a seminar I taught in Venezuela tells another story about cultural differences in driving. The student had recently vacationed in Germany. As her German hosts drove their car on the outskirts of a small town late one night the driver insisted on waiting for a red light to change at an obscure intersection where no cars could be seen for miles. Coming from a culture where official rules are much more open to creative interpretation, the Venezuelan simply could not comprehend why the driver wouldn't just drive through the red light. This clash of cultures doesn't end there. German law also forbids anyone to sit in a car without fastening the seatbelt, even when the vehicle is parked and the engine is turned off. Cultures are characterized not only by their official rules and unofficial, informal rules, but also by patterned ways of obeying and breaking rules.

Motivations for breaking rules, and the behavioral patterns that result, are greatly influenced by relationships between prescribing authorities and rule users/breakers. Vehicle drivers in Rio run red lights partly because they don't much respect the government that put the lights there in the first place. Traffic semaphores in Brazil often appear in extremely illogical places, reminding drivers of the institutional incompetence against which they rebel generally in daily life. In Brazil, traffic lights signal institutional incompetence as much as they do traffic flows. The police are as likely as anyone else to break the official rules. Sometimes prevailing rules are based more on the relationship between enforcers and violators than between the civil state and rule breakers. In Florence, Italy, for example, African street vendors must pick up their illegal displays of sunglasses, African hats, and trinkets and move when the police drive by, only to put their wares back on the exact same spot immediately after the authorities leave. The vendors even smile and wave at the police as they feign concern. Thus, the rule against street vending is not enforced, but a rule that demands symbolic respect for the enforcing authorities must be superficially obeyed as part of a game of social power. The clash between official rules and rules-in-use can have far-reaching political and cultural implications. In China and the former communist nations of Europe, for example, people have realized that government officials at the highest level don't play by the rules of social equality that they themselves have set. This double standard is commonly interpreted as a profound breach of ethics which implicitly encourages rule breaking and corruption at all social levels and a total mistrust of government, its laws and decrees.

Rules are interpreted situationally in all cultures. To behave strictly according to literal rules carries the risk of becoming a "judgmental dope" rather than a "competent rule user" (Garfinkel, 1967). Every use of a rule is an interpretation of the rule. As Edgerton points out, creative uses of rules are often motivated by self-interest. He calls this motivated involvement with rules "strategic interactionism." People make the best use of rules for their self-interest, or in the interest of their social affiliations, depending on the situation (Edgerton, 1985: 13). Obeying official rules or going along with commonly accepted ways of doing things is but one option. Rules are more than requirements, restraints, and instructions. They are schemata people use to choose particular courses of action.

The choices that are made, and the forms of social interaction that are created, however, are not random or democratic. While strategic interactionism (or "tactical rules;" see Lull, 1990) rightly emphasizes the plasticity of rules and the creative undertakings of individual rule users, normative rules in particular also have an undeniable ability to shape consciousness and influence social activity. Together with the concept of choice – which speaks to the interpretative freedom, imagination, and creativity of rule users – we must, therefore, also take up the concept of power located in the statuses and roles of rule makers and articulators. We need to know who prescribes what ideas and actions and how the prescriptive force of rules relates to socioeconomic conditions. The structural contours of a society, and the social formations contained within them, necessarily reflect material and ideological relations wherein power is a central feature. Rules representing institutionalized sources of power are one important type of rule, therefore, and power is the topic to which we now turn.

Power

Rules legitimate, shape, and facilitate dominant ideologies (chapter 1) by linking ideological representations with authority. This is the essence of many social rules – the constitution and coordination of specific thoughts and courses of action representing motivated agendas that imply particular ideological inclinations and rely on the credibility of institutional authority for their effectiveness. Rules simultaneously manifest and reinforce authority. But as I hope to have already shown, rules gain legitimacy and prescriptive force not only from their embeddedness in structures of authority or from their hegemonic relation with other institutions. To be effective, rules must also be perceived by social actors as emotionally satisfying, culturally relevant, socially useful, or otherwise appealing.

The power of rules, therefore, cannot easily be categorized or generalized. Their influence does not resemble traditional definitions of power such as "the capability of an individual or group to exert its will over others" (Giddens, 1991: 211). The exercise of rule-based power is not unidirectional and its consequences do not necessarily oppress others. People frequently find rule structures comforting. Most children want rules and enforcement so they feel noticed and loved. Employees want to know workplace rules so they can comply to insure their security. The faithful willingly obey religious codes. Consumers look for guidance.

Rules promote explicit and implicit understandings that inspire patterns of social behavior. But we must distinguish between rules and behavioral patterns. Rules are *not* the behavioral patterns themselves; they are cognitive and emotional frames of reference that encourage construction and maintenance of certain patterns. The patterns take shape in routine communication. The resulting patterns are *conventions* which then themselves assume prescriptive force as *social norms* (Shimanoff, 1980: 110). Convention refers to conventional behavior. Norm prescribes what should be done. To summarize the process, rules are concretized in routine communicative interaction. The resulting behavioral patterns, stimulated and shaped by both personal and mediated communication, become social conventions that reflect underlying ideational image systems structured and advocated by rules. Conventions are then often prescriptively interpreted as social norms. Thus, rules help stimulate particular patterns of social interaction (conventions), which, in turn, reinforce the rules (as norms), compounding and repeating the cycle of influence.

Drawing from the work of musicologist Charles Hamm (1983), let me show how this works with an example from the spiritual politics of colonial America. Eighteenth century psalms sung by enthusiastic members of early American religious congregations at first produced a heterophonous clashing of sounds. To impose order on the situation, religious leaders created songbooks. The songbooks instructed everyone to sing the same notes and words simultaneously, thereby establishing social conformity in the form of a particular type of ritualistic communication – a literal chorus of voices organized on terms set by an agent of institutional religious authority. The church service itself was also structured so that singing could take place only at certain times. A member of the church was thus required to conform to a set of imposed rules comprising the singing of psalms and the conduct of a religious service. These coordinated performances combined to form a sanctioned, structured social convention that systematically introduced institutionally based, rule-governed norms to new members. By defining what is normal in the form and content of the church service, religious leaders were able to institutionalize ideology while asserting their authority by imposing and maintaining rules. This example represents but one of many ideological domains (spirituality), institutions (organized religion), and agencies (the Puritan Church).

Key to the influence of rules, then, is their homology with ideological predispositions and sources of authority. Furthermore, rules supply references for the ongoing construction of meaning and development of social relations based on configurations and syntheses that have already been made. So, as we have just seen, to join in ritualistic religious activity, or to participate in any other even mildly organized social behavior for that matter, presumes at least tacit involvement in reproducing the ideological assumptions that make up the activity.

The very status of "rule" can be authoritative. We have all heard the simple retort "because it's the rule!" or "because that's the way things are done around here" (from a convention to a norm; from a description "of" behavior to a prescription "for" behavior; see Kratochwil, 1989) to justify a policy or action. Although rules themselves do not *explain* policies or behaviors, they are often used to rationalize activity or invoke authority, as in the case of a father who instructs his child to do something, "because I say so, that's why!" We often quickly discover who has the power to set and enforce rules locally. More distant rulers are often less identifiable.

Lines of authority

> I'm sure the parents of these children think it's cute, but I can assure you that most people don't appreciate being instructed by a four year-old! (from a letter appearing in Ann Landers's syndicated newspaper advice column about the practice of using children's voices on recorded telephone answering machine messages)

Tracing lines of authority in rule formation, articulation, and enforcement reveals much about social hierarchies and their forms of power. These hierarchies can be headed by an individual strong man or woman, social coalitions of various types, or larger, more abstract and encompassing sources. In its most basic form, rule-governing authority is biologically conditioned. The world heavy-weight boxing champion, for instance, can mightily influence his social world by using brute force to impose his will (at least until another more powerful institution, constitutional law, intervenes and puts him in jail for doing just that, as was Mike Tyson's fate). Male heads of the household, elders, older siblings, and strong persons of many other types impose and maintain order in their zones of influence. Patriarchy in societies all over the world evolved from roles developed in premodern cultures where men's superior physical size and musculature, together with women's biological role as childbearer, led to a gendered division of labor that is still with us. Males became procurers and protectors required to engage the world outside the family. Such profound responsibilities also gave them relatively greater autonomy and opportunity. This division of labor led to development of restricted social roles for both sexes and the creation of differences in power that are more favorable to men in some important ways.

Hierarchies of authority originating in biological difference extend deeply into the public sphere. Men dominate economic, political, and religious institutions everywhere today, often bringing competition and conflict with them. Unfortunately, as Anthony Giddens bluntly points out, it seems that "men's attitude toward the world is essentially an instrumental one, based on domination and manipulation" (1991: 229). Presidents of large, technologically advanced nations can impose military force on lesser powers, or on their own people when an uprising occurs, thereby exercising a form of institutionalized patriarchy. Religious leaders are almost always men who, in their own spheres and with a somewhat more gentle touch, command their congregations. Chief executive officers of corporations are respected mainly because of their organizational status and power. Fathers impose their will at home. All these individuals operate within and are legitimated by ideological institutions and agencies – politics, religion, business, family. The rules they articulate influence their environments in part simply because the institutions and agencies they represent remain in place and continue to operate.

In today's industrialized and post-industrial societies, many of the most powerful social organizations – transnational corporations, for instance – are utterly faceless (except, perhaps, for their corporate media spokesmen and women – actors, actresses, sports personalities, etc., whose authority springs from the world of popular, not corporate, culture). Some of these agencies, IBM is a prime example, even require dress codes to guarantee an anonymous appearance – the infamous "corporate look." The military, of course, takes this thinking to the extreme. Although all social institutions have their temporarily visible personalities, we have been taught to respect "the company," "the church," "the school," "the union," "the army," "the party," and "the law," for example, as legitmate originators, articulators, and enforcers of rules. In many realms of the modern world, our trust is no longer so much in personal acquaintances as it is in social institutions and images. It is trust "in a general system of expectations" (Kratochwil, 1989: 114) and in the abstract capacities of expert knowledge emanating from a host of distant authorities. This kind of trust is clearly evident every time we step into an airplane, for example (Giddens, 1990: 26).

The special authority of electronic media

Radio and television studios and transmitters are among the most valued and protected technical facilities anywhere in the world. Most commercial broadcast stations are enormously profitable; being granted permission to transmit is said to be like having a license to print money. In nations suffering political unrest, government leaders often try to control broadcast facilities militarily. They fear that a takeover of telecommunications installations by revolutionary groups would signal a most serious challenge to political authority. Such a takeover can greatly heighten social anxiety, perhaps causing the administration to fall from power. One action taken by the communist government in the People's Republic of China during the 1989 student and worker uprising, for instance, was to impose martial law and seize control of all mass media facilities. In cases such as this, forces that control the electronic media control the country.

The idea of *mass communication* is indeed a weighty sociological concept. Though audiences certainly do not respond to media messages as an undifferentiated mass (as was the early theory; see Wright, 1960, for example), ownership and control of the mass media, especially the electronic media, are unparalleled forms of social power even in the most stable societies. Electronic media are among the modern world's most celebrated and effective conveyers of ideology and articulators of social rules. Media stimulate short-term patterns and long-term conventions that can affect an entire society. Growth in profits attributable to commercial advertising, children reciting themes from television programs, increases in the attendance of live performances given by popular music artists following the airing of a hit record on radio and MTV, even the very attendance by a national audience to a television program are all examples of media influence.

People in the more developed countries especially tend to be critical, even quite cynical, about the mass media, particularly television programs, commercials, and the practice of journalism. Still, the mass media are among the most potent of modern-day authorities. The vast majority of people in highly developed countries all over the world, for example, say they trust television more than any other source of information. Television wins the credibility contest because it is visual, immediate, and convenient (so that it is used habitually, fostering a special kind of trust). Furthermore, television's credibility as a medium interacts with the interpersonal credibility of its personalities. Technological capability and personal ethos coalesce to create unequalled institutional legitimacy. The most famous example of this combined authority may be the influence American newscaster Walter Cronkite enjoyed on CBS television for many years. His unsurpassed personal credibility and the widespread public acceptance of television as the most believable news medium worked together to inspire the confidence of millions of viewers. When he signed off every evening with "And that's the way it was this day," Cronkite had effectively circumscribed the world's events into a half-hour capsule gently given to an adoring audience who deeply trusted his fatherly image.

Cronkite's legendary popularity can help us understand other ways the mass media are patriarchal authorities. In a sense, the electronic media are extensions of male culture. They were invented by men. The first voices to be heard on radio were those of engineers transmitting signals by tinkering with the tubes and wires. It didn't take long for another male-dominated institution, commerce, to recognize and capitalize on the profit potential of radio once it became technically feasible. Television, following the successful precedent of radio, was born a commercial medium. As a consequence of this marriage between engineering and commerce, males became the first owners, managers, programmers, technicians, regulators, and personalities on radio and television. The electronic media today continue to extend and amplify male authority in even the most subtle ways. To cite but one telling example, more than 90 percent of television "voice overs" (when a disembodied voice is heard over the visuals of a commercial) are done by men, asserting masculine authority in a way that is unlikely to be consciously perceived or criticized by viewers. Institutional voices, especially those of the mass media, are indeed loud and clear. The special authority of electronic media, asserting and reinforcing endless streams of ideologically charged information, is, without question, an impressive social force.

Public images and private practices: media, rules, and the macro/micro question

Electronic media play an especially influential role in contemporary rule-governed interaction. Media help shape and maintain rules and the ideological predispositions underlying them because their unique and powerful technical capabilities and appealing content are the most effective means of information diffusion ever invented. Mass media traverse not only geographic frontiers, but also boundaries of class, race, culture, politics, education, and gender to distribute entertainment and information that instill and refresh particular points of view and ways of making sense as a routine product of transmission. By articulating ideological syntheses that promote certain perspectives and exclude others, and by relating ideological inflections to sources of authority, the mass media help constitute and regulate social reality by structuring some of their audiences' most common and important experiences.

Rules commute from sweeping macrosocial environments, through various mid-range configurations, to the very smallest, most idiosyncratic contexts and activities. Rules link public agendas with private worlds. Some rules promote patterns of thought and social activity in ways that define large populations. But familiar surroundings such as living spaces, workplaces, and social gathering spots of all kinds are likewise structured and governed by rules, some deriving from distant authority, others more local. Of interest is the fluidity of rules across sociocultural contexts, from macro to micro and the reverse, and the ways rules are interpreted and used as they move from place to place.

This crossing and intermeshing of social arenas and circumstances helps us understand how rules are put to work by their originators, articulators, enforcers, and interpreter-users.

Mass media help break down distance between the macrosocial and the microsocial. They bring public themes into private environments where they enter into and are influenced by local conditions, orientations, authorities, and practices. The public sphere has been mediated and reconstituted in the electronic age (Thompson, 1994), both technologically and socially. News is a clear example. As Anthony Giddens points out, "distant events may become as familiar, or more so, than proximate influences, and integrated into frameworks of personal experience" (1984: 189). The same can be said of virtually all electronic media content. Employing media imagery in the routine construction of interpersonal discourses of all kinds is a common social use of television. But what appears on the mass media is useful not only because it is so available and appealing. Media consumers' own interests, exercised within the circumstances and venues of reception (the endless microsocial contexts), greatly influence how media imagery is interpreted and used too.

Private involvement with structured public discourses ranges from willing compliance to radical resistance. The influence of television in China illustrates the point. No doubt, Chinese Communist Party ideology is supported by a sizeable proportion of the overall population, especially lesser educated people and rural dwellers. But many other people firmly reject the didactic propaganda disseminated by state institutions, including the mass media. The 1989 student-worker uprising in Beijing was motivated in part by just such resistance to official ideology and culture. In China, what might seem at first to be iron-clad, monolithic, non-negotiable rules that dictate ideology and social behavior have in practice become explicit resources for the construction of an alternative consciousness and the imagination of a very different future.

Explicit and implicit rules help organize social behavior by connecting ideology to authority. Chinese communist ideology during the past decade, for instance, introduced and promoted two principal ideas: modernization and reform. The government used all its communication resources to articulate official definitions and mandate compliance with national objectives. Modernization referred to China's necessity to extensively upgrade four major areas: agriculture, industry, science/technology, and national defense. Reform was to be the means for successful modernization. Both modernization and reform definitively linked dominant ideology with prevailing authority – an association considered to be vital to state control. But what actually happened when the government tried to put the prescriptions into effect? Modernization and reform became rule-based ideological resources that were used by people whose intentions differed greatly from the authors of the original, official plans. Resistance first germinated inside China's social institutions where professionals had their own ideas about the direction China should be headed. As I pointed out in my own research on China:

> many of the ideological twists and turns that have come from the national government itself for the past several years in China have been influenced by nuances originating with workers in television and the other mass media who have dared to author unofficial ideas, accounts, and explanations. By invoking the government's own rhetoric and rationale of openness and reform, China's change agents in the media have actually been able to do their oppositional work in the guise of sanctioned national interest. (Lull, 1991: 213)

The media audience helped invent an alternative modernization and reform too, sometimes by converting official expressions. Many Chinese people ridicule and otherwise resist the teacherly, misleading, overblown dominant ideology of government propaganda. They detest the Communist Party's simple-minded self-promotion, its blatantly biased news reports, the laughable TV "model worker" programs, the many exaggerated advertising claims made about domestic products, and the unavailability of advertised foreign goods. Viewers watch TV with hypercritical sensitivity. For instance, several family members we interviewed in China told us they completely ignore the official narration which accompanies stories on TV newscasts and focus their attention instead on the attractive visuals. What really struck many Chinese about a televised visit Deng Xiaoping made to Tokyo, for example, was not the trade agreement the Chinese leader consummated with the Japanese, or the pomp and circumstance surrounding Deng's foreign travel, but the modern skyscrapers, cars, fashions, and busy lifestyles Japanese people obviously have. A television drama imported from Japan was interpreted by Chinese viewers mainly in terms of the free-market economic opportunities enjoyed by the lead character, Oshin. A 12-part political TV drama written and produced inside China (*New Star*) was interpreted by most people nationwide as a radical critique of communist bureaucracy and corruption, not as a plan for future leadership, the official intention. One viewer questioned how communism could be better than capitalism when imported American TV shows taught her that "in the West, even terrible people can own cars!" Almost no one in China owns a car.

Resistance is sharpest when overall conditions encourage and frame such alternative ideological conversions. The economic depression, political repression, and cultural suffocation suffered by people under communist rule in the latter part of the twentieth century created tremendous social unrest. Communism came to be regarded by many people as an overdetermined set of ideological and cultural rules prescribing an even bleaker future. Media technology and content thus became pervasive, salient resources for resistance, both inside social institutions where media professionals exercise some degree of autonomy, and outside where audience members form their own opinions and coalitions of opposition in response to official agendas. The television audience has rejected the blatant propaganda while it is attracted to (often extremely idealized) representations of alternative cultural worlds presented on the very same media.

Such breaks with authority are not always so dramatic, violent, or far from home. Consider, for example, the plight of the Catholic Church today. A Gallup poll recently reported that the vast majority of American Catholics believe married couples should be able to choose whatever form of birth control they want, including abortion if necessary. Most Catholics in the United States also favor the idea of women priests and the right of priests to marry. These profound disagreements with papal positions and rules reflect the limited choices people have at the official level. But Catholics make their own Catholicism – everywhere. To the horror of the Pope, for example, Latin American Catholics have invented various local religions composed of Vatican dogma and liturgy, but also of local customs, beliefs, superstitions, and rituals, including African voodoo rites. Many Brazilians, for instance, believe in the church at an abstract, spiritual level, but adapt and transform Catholic ideology, authority, rules, and rituals to fit their own personal inclinations and cultural preferences. Social movements like those we see in China and Latin America are but two examples of the "massive areas of collective appropriation" (Giddens, 1991: 175) we see in the world today.

Rules in perspective

Pervasive and powerful as they are, rules certainly don't cause or explain everything. Basic reflexes, survival instincts, spontaneous emotional outbursts, and unthinking conditioned behavior, for example, need not be required or suggested by rules. Various social theorists, even counting among them those who embrace the concept of rule as a fundamental social organizing principle, find substantial domains of activity where they believe rules don't apply. One viewpoint, for instance, is that utterly pragmatic behavior is not governed by rules. Roger Lindsay argues that "the regularities in the way a man goes to work are a product of the interaction between his ability to solve spatial problems and his desire to reach his goal" (1977: 165). Friedrich V. Kratochwil makes a distinction between rules and values: he claims that "rules ... prescribe specific *actions*, [while] values inform the *attitudes* of [social] actors ... and influence our choices largely by evoking emotional attachments rather than through the readily available cognitive patterns characteristic of rules" (1989: 64). Willard Quine draws the line at the issue of conscious awareness, arguing that "behavior is not guided by a rule unless the behaver knows are rule and can state it" (1972: 27).

The diversity represented in the evaluations of rules indicates, first of all, an overriding lack of consensus on what rules really are. But beyond this, to imagine that rules theory or any other perspective could provide a sufficient explanation of social behavior can only be a misguided pipe-dream. I agree with some of the assessments raised in the previous paragraph and disagree with others.

To my way of thinking, for example, emotional as well as cognitive qualities are absolutely fundamental to rules. And I certainly can't imagine conceptualizing rules only as formally articulated or consciously realized. Finally, I insist that it is simply not useful to think of rules as causes of social behavior. To follow, disobey, ignore, reformulate, or appropriate a rule and its underlying structures of thought and authority is not a cause-and-effect process, but a choice made by individuals and groups in particular contexts, sometimes for reasons we may never fully understand. Nonetheless, to conceptualize social interaction in terms of rules is a productive way to theorize the intricate relation between ideology, authority, and power. By no means does the story of social influence end there. An extremely unruly force, culture, has its role to play too.

3
Culture and Cultural Power

Years ago Raymond Williams (1962) succinctly defined culture as "a particular way of life" shaped by values, traditions, beliefs, material objects, and territory. Culture is a complex and dynamic ecology of people, things, world views, activities, and settings that fundamentally endures but is also changed in routine communication and social interaction. Culture is context. It's how we talk and dress, the food we eat and how we prepare and consume it, the gods we invent and the ways we worship them, how we divide up time and space, how we dance, the values to which we socialize our children, and all the other details that make up everyday life. This perspective on culture implies that no culture is inherently superior to any other and that cultural richness by no means derives from economic standing. Culture as everyday life is a steadfastly democratic idea.[1]

Today familiar resources ranging from food, language, and religious rituals to TV programs and popular music are combined by individuals and groups into distinctive cultural repertoires or "tool kits" (Hannerz, 1969) used to fashion contemporary habits, skills, styles, and "strategies of action" (Swidler, 1986). The particular ways of life we encounter and the strategies of action we devise nowadays are composed of a vastly expanded and differentiated pool of cultural resources. The flood of symbolic imagery ushered in especially by telecommunications technology in the late twentieth century has led to radical changes worldwide in the cultural syntheses people make. More than ever before, constructing and organizing everyday life is quintessential interpretative activity (Geertz, 1973).

Race and class

Culture and race are not the same thing, but they are often associated or confused with one another. This is understandable because, particularly in premodern times, characteristic ways of living reflected shared, relatively exclusive geographic territories traceable to racial origins. When we say, for example, "Chinese culture," we refer to an imagined people and way of life originating in race and geography. Europeans have long marked cultural differences according to geographic (national) boundaries. Today, however, racial and geopolitical definitions of culture, while they still strongly persist, are becoming far more complex and ambiguous. The extraordinary transmigration of peoples from one corner of the earth to another and the explosive proliferation of the mass media combine to dramatically alter the ethnic and territorial fixity of culture. According to United Nations statistics, for instance, more than 100 million people were living outside their country of origin by 1993, a 100 percent increase in just three years.

Culture is grounded not only in race, but in social class. Race and class are intimately intertwined, but their linkage is often overlooked in cultural analysis. Thus to speak of, say, Korean culture might bring to mind a stereotypical or idealized image that can easily obscure how differently rich Koreans live from poor Koreans in many respects. If culture takes form in everyday life, and if the everyday lives of the rich and poor differ – even among people who descend from the same racial lines and live close to one another – then culture is differentiated meaningfully by social class. Said another way, a person's ranking in the socioeconomic hierarchy is not just a financial status, but a cultural demarcation as well. This hierarchical relationship between social structure and culture has been well recognized in classical Marxist theory. The crux of the typical Marxist argument is that because "culture is determined by forces outside itself, [it] does not have autonomy in the causal sense" (Alexander and Seidman, 1990: 2). From Daniel Bell to Jürgen Habermas, culture historically has been subverted to social structure in the writings of many critical theorists (Archer, 1990).

Culture is indeed structured in various ways, some of them owing to differences in social class, but it certainly is not determined by material relations or social class positions. Nor is culture of secondary importance. Such a view doesn't take into account the variety and scope of culture, including its brazen contradictions. Any theory of culture as determined by outside forces fails to recognize the vital, creative ways people produce culture in the routine undertakings of their daily lives. Culture, therefore, should not be considered something "simply derived from class, as if it were a crude form of ideology" (Rowe and Schelling, 1991: 9). We need a less parochial critical perspective. As Martín-Barbero observes, "an impatience to explain away cultural differences as class differences prevented Marxism from analyzing the specificity of the conflicts that articulate a culture and the modes of struggle that produce a given culture" (1993: 20).

Social theorists and researchers have in fact wrestled with the complex connection between social structure and culture for years. In sociology and communication, for example, some scholars have tried to explain why people of various social classes prefer different genres within cultural domains such as art and music. Why, for instance, does one young Brazilian prefer samba music while another would much rather listen to hard rock? To explain such differences, American sociologist Herbert Gans tried to accommodate both social class and culture within a concept he calls "taste culture." Taste culture refers to *cultural strata* in a society that approximate the *social class strata* of that society. While Gans does not equate the two, he finds significant parallels between taste and social class position. A simple illustration is that people from the upper socioeconomic classes prefer classical music more than do members of the lower classes (Gans, 1974). Such relationships between social class and taste, however, rarely correspond so neatly as they do in this example. Although they may have more in common culturally than just musical taste, fans of heavy metal, rap, rock, punk, jazz, and even country and western music, for instance, cannot easily be grouped socioeconomically. And to return to the samba/hard-rock example: in Brazil, samba is identified with youth from the lower socioeconomic classes and hard rock with the upper classes, while in Europe and North America (where samba music has been appropriated as an exotic cultural form) just the opposite is true. George H. Lewis has productively elaborated Gans' notion by explaining taste cultures in terms grounded not solely in social class positions. Lewis (1992) shows how in the preferences people have for types of music ranging from rap to country and western, taste also links up with demographic factors, aesthetic orientations, and political considerations.

Habitus

Certainly the most systematic and sophisticated effort to come to grips theoretically with the problematic relationship between cultural taste and social structure is the research and writing of the French sociologist Pierre Bourdieu (1984; 1990a; 1990b; 1993). Bourdieu resurrected and reworked the idea of *habitus* to signify *a system of socially learned cultural predispositions and activities that differentiate people by their lifestyles*. Habitus encompasses the whole gamut of cultural activity – the production, perception, and evaluation of everyday practices (1990a: 131). While habitus is claimed to account for taste, it is not simply a cold system of aesthetics detached from the sensate world; habitus pervades our bodies as well as our minds.

According to Bourdieu, cultural comfort zones and characteristic ways of acting are learned through social experience. But while people may "internalize their position in social space" (1990a: 110), these experiences are not determined by and do not perfectly reflect one's slot on a socioeconomic scale. Social space is made in social practice, and practice is not determined by social structure. What a person learns culturally is influenced by, but not limited to, the tastes and everyday activities of people who occupy the same social class. Furthermore, social experience is not straightforward learning. We don't acquire cultural orientations and competencies by merely imitating our environments. Bourdieu describes the subtle process of sociocultural learning with a well-known metaphor from the world of sports. He believes habitus develops in a manner similar to the way athletes acquire knowledge and strategies in sport by means of their "feel for the game." Especially in constant action sports such as football (soccer) or basketball, veteran players know what to do almost instinctively. Like playing a sport competently, cultural skills and styles become second nature. You know what to do, even without thinking about it, based on accumulated knowledge. The feel for the cultural game develops from motivated, strategic, repeated, practical experience. In this way habitus becomes "a system of acquired dispositions" and an "organizing principle of action" (1990a: 13).

Habitus is a logic of taste following from a logic of practice in social interaction, according to Bourdieu, but such activity involves much more than simply carrying out or obeying social rules. The system of dispositions which makes up the habitus has a generative quality in much the same way that language does (Chomsky, 1972). Cultural orientations, like languages, are open systems whose particular forms, styles, and meanings are constantly created, reinforced, and transcended (i.e. "generated") in actual use. The generative nature of habitus underscores several key theoretical assertions Bourdieu offers: social actors are purposive, active agents who do not blindly reproduce culture; modes of behavior making up the habitus are patterned but not finely regular or lawful; and part of the system of dispositions and practical logic of habitus is "vagueness," which assures that spontaneity and improvisation will characterize people's "ordinary relations to the world" (1990a: 78). The indeterminate, generative, and vague qualities of habitus reflect its contingent nature. Habitus is not a person's or a group's unified cultural style that applies uniformly in all situations, but is instead acquired and exercised uniquely in relation to different cultural territories, domains, or "fields" (Bourdieu, 1993).

Money really isn't everything: symbolic and cultural power

We should have gotten our freedom much sooner;
You ain't never seen a black man on *The Honeymooners*.
(lyrics from "Back on the Block" by Quincy Jones; *The Honeymooners* is a famous 1950s American TV serial)

Power takes many forms. As John B. Thompson (1994) points out, *economic power* is institutionalized in industry and commerce; *political power* is institutionalized in the state apparatus; *coercive power* is institutionalized in military and paramilitary organizations. Without doubt, the power of these institutions is based largely on their ability to establish, maintain, and enforce certain types of social rules. But *symbolic power*, which is of great interest to us here, is far more ephemeral, plastic, and democratic. Symbolic power can be defined as "the capacity to use symbolic forms . . . to intervene in and influence the course of action or events" (Thompson, 1994). This kind of power is sometimes institutionalized as well; the obvious example is the communicative capacity of mass media organizations.[2] But symbolic power and its correlate *cultural power*, deriving from the tactical undertakings of social actors constructing their everyday lives, are not exercised solely by social institutions. Symbolic and cultural power are far more accessible and usable than are economic, political, and coercive power. They are central to daily life, helping us create, cope with, adapt to, and transform environments structured by forces of economic, political, and military authority.

The commercial mass media have greatly accelerated and diversified the influence of cultural power. By cultural power I mean *the ability to define a situation culturally*. Cultural power is the ability of individuals and groups to produce meanings and to construct (usually partial and temporary) ways of life (or constellations of "cultural zones") that appeal to the senses, emotions, and thoughts of the self and others. It resembles what Anthony Giddens calls "life politics . . . a politics of choice . . . of lifestyle . . . of life decisions" (1991: 214). Although cultural power has certain deep-felt economic and political origins, dimensions, and consequences, it is not the same as economic or political power, nor is it produced only by the already powerful. Being a successful cultural programmer in the competitive cultural marketplace engenders other unique roles, statuses, and achievements.

Cultural power interacts with and assimilates symbolic power (Thompson, 1994) because culture today comprises not only the traditional values, durable features, and routine activities that make up local living environments, but also a broad and attractive array of symbolic resources expressed by the mass media and other social institutions. People routinely select and weave mediated, publicly available symbolic representations and discourses into the particular cultural discourses of their everyday lives, producing what Joli Jensen calls "culturalconversations . . . particular modes of social organization" (1990: 182). The cultural "feel for the game" Bourdieu describes must today also take into account technologically mediated experiences and literacies. Cultural power is exercised when people use symbolic displays, including the systemic ideological and cultural associations, structures of authority, and rules that underlie them, in their cultural strategies of action. True enough, mediated symbolic images are made powerful culturally first by the way their sponsoring institutions organize and present them. But, ultimately, cultural power reflects how, in the situated realms of everyday life, individuals and groups construct and declare their cultural identities and activities and how those expressions and behaviors influence others.

People's culture

The term "popular culture" (*cultura popular*) in Spanish and Portuguese means literally "the culture of the people" (*de la gente, del pueblo; da gente, do povo*). Popular, in this sense, does not signify widespread, mainstream, dominant, or commercially successful. In Latin languages and cultures it refers much more to the idea that culture develops from the creativity of ordinary people. Popular culture comes from people; it is not given to them. This perspective tears away at distinctions between producers and consumers of cultural artifacts, between culture industries and contexts of reception. We all produce popular culture. Constructing popular culture is an exercise in cultural power.

Cultural studies theorist John Fiske (1989) takes up the relationship between popular culture and cultural power when he discusses how artifacts ranging from blue jeans to Madonna are variously interpreted and used tactically by fans in ways that suit their particular interests. But Fiske carries the matter one controversial step further. He argues that popular culture is never dominant because "it is formed always in reaction to, and never as part of, the forces of domination" (p. 43). Making popular culture, according to Fiske, is social struggle. Contrary to the more frequently made criticism that popular culture is nothing but capitalistic commercial exploitation or "mass culture," Fiske argues that the making of popular culture is resistance to and evasion from dominant ideological and cultural forces: "Popular pleasures must always be those of the oppressed, they must contain elements of the oppositional, the evasive, the scandalous, the offensive, the vulgar, the resistant. Pleasures offered by ideological conformity are muted and hegemonic; they are not popular pleasures and work in opposition to them" (p. 127). Popular culture, thus, is empowering. The mass media contribute to the process by distributing cultural resources to oppressed individuals and subordinate groups which they use to construct their tactics of resistance against hegemonic strategies of containment. One of Fiske's sharpest examples of this is how young Australian Aborigines who watch old American TV westerns ally themselves with the Indians and "cheer them on as they attack the wagon train or homestead, killing the white men and carrying off the white women" (p. 25).

Suite culture and street culture: of institutions and audiences

The ability of media to spotlight and disseminate ideological and cultural fragments first of all answers the often asked question, "Do the mass media reflect social reality or create it?" Without doubt, the answer is "both." More interesting questions are, "*How* do the media reflect and create social reality, who benefits, and in what ways?" Or perhaps even more to the point, "How do the media help facilitate the social construction of cultural reality?" Technically, of course, the mass media can neither reflect nor construct sociocultural reality as no such pure or permanent thing exists anyway. Furthermore, media programmers have no interest in reflecting or creating reality. What they do instead is piece together symbolic fragments to produce stories that resemble our surroundings in some ways and not in others. Commercial television, for instance, presents imagery that ranges from news, documentaries, and "reality" programs to total fantasy, frothiness, and absurdity. There is no commitment to faithfully produce anything except that which quickly catches the public's fantasy and turns at least a short-term profit. In developing prime-time commercial television programs, for instance, producers, network officials, station executives, and advertisers all try to research and ultimately guess what the audience will watch.[3] The chosen content is packaged and put on trial. Certain themes, genres, styles, and stars strike a responsive chord, resonating with audience members' identities, emotions, opinions, tastes, and ambitions. The "popular" in popular culture thus really means that cultural impulses and images originate in everyday environments and are later attended to, interpreted, and used by ordinary people – sometimes, but not always, in very resistant ways – after being commodified and circulated by the culture industries and mass media.

The social circulation of media images surely helps bring about commercial success and makes possible the spread of dominant ideology (see chapter 1). But, as we have seen, what catches on in television and the rest of commercial culture – especially film and music – also become widely recognized, accessible resources used by audiences to exercise cultural power. Many of the most profound social consequences of popular culture – both in favor of and resistant to dominant modes of thought – lie precisely in people's uses of media imagery to express themselves and influence others. Images appearing on the mass media in capitalist economies are mustered institutionally to promote particular products, help create communities of consumption for product groups and brand names, and generally reinforce a consumerist atmosphere. Such institutional priorities and forms of cultural packaging, however, do not stifle the cultural creativity of audience members.

On the contrary, they inspire it. Underlying all media images is cultural authority. The media routinely promote cultural authors who capture the imagination of audiences because their ways of thinking, acting, and being are presented so attractively. Audience members identify with what those images can mean and put the cultural representations to work in their everyday living situations. So while the sights and sounds of mass-mediated popular culture are distributed by commercial enterprises headquartered in the entertainment capitals of the world, they can be put to use by anyone operating in even the most remote provinces. Cultural power is exercised by individual as well as institutional "sponsors."

A fundamental motivation explaining certain human behavior is the desire for material goods. This may seem to be an overly simplistic, uncritical point, but its importance cannot be overstated. People everywhere want "stuff." Consumer goods and imagery are indispensable resources which drive and change culture. As Paul Willis points out, the market stimulates a "permanent and contradictory revolution in every culture which sweeps away old limits and dependencies" (1990: 26). The predispositions and social practices that make up the cultural habitus theorized by Bourdieu, for instance, are constructed in large measure from symbolic and material resources of the commercial market. These resources are not shapeless, but they are not determining either. In forming the preferences, opinions, and tastes of habitus, social actors discover that "the world is not presented as pure chaos, totally devoid of necessity and capable of being constructed in any old way. But this world does not present itself as totally structured either, or as capable of imposing on every perceiving subject the principles of its own construction" (Bourdieu, 1990a: 132).

An extraordinary example of the correspondence between production and consumption, between ideological representation and social interpretation, between symbolic power and cultural power, is the American athletic shoe phenomenon which had reached worldwide proportions by the 1990s. Many American athletes, especially professional basketball stars, have been recruited to hype the expensive shoes in commercial TV advertising. Michael Jordan's and Scottie Pippen's campaigns for Nike athletic shoes are particularly striking. These commercials are stunning cultural displays. The sleek, graceful black man soars into mid-air, defying gravity as he stays aloft for several long seconds. He is sentimentally embraced by an ultra-slow-motion camera and editing techniques that fuse one spectacular, dream-like image to the next. Customized music and audio effects further enhance the body performance. The storyline of the basketball-star/black-culture/athletic-shoe commercials often is a series of solo slam-dunks – when the player leaps high and violently jams the ball directly through the metal hoop (a perfect metaphor for aggressive sex). Anonymous (usually white) men stand confused and helpless as they watch the cultural colonizers fly over them.[4] Sometimes the bystanders are shown in pathetic attempts to copy the black athletes' superhuman feats. At the end of the commercial the shoe company's logo appears, accompanied by a slogan such as Nike's famous and tantalizingly ambiguous "Just Do It!"[5]

Jordan and Pippen project not only awesome physical ability, but cultural power and authority on behalf of their sponsors. Their presence contributes mightily to the multibillion-dollar athletic shoe industry. But profits generated from the commercials are not all institutional and not all paid in dollars. Inner-city culture is intensely glorified in many athletic shoe commercials. The black, inner-city playground, rough as it is, has become the cultural reference point indicating where the really good basketball players come from. Some of the commercials are filmed in black and white to further accent the stark quality of the "hood." The marketing technique is to transfer images of the culturally constituted world, the ghetto playground, to the consumer product, the shoes. The commodity is resignified through cultural space. Grant McCracken argues that:

> The creative director of an advertising agency seeks to join [the culturally constituted world and the consumer product] in such a way that the viewer/reader glimpses an essential similarity between them. When this symbolic equivalence is successfully established, the viewer/reader attributes certain properties he or she knows to exist in the culturally constituted world to the consumer good. The known properties of the world thus come to be resident in the unknown properties of the consumer good. The transfer of meaning from world to good is accomplished. (1990: 77)

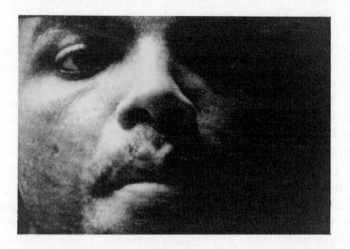

Photo 3.1   Attitude. Bad boy Charles Barkley tells parents that just because he dunks a basketball doesn't mean he has to accept responsibility for their children: "I ain't no role model!" is the theme of this Nike TV ad (reprinted with permission of Nike, Inc.)

Athletic shoe commercials not only lionize black turf, they validate one cultural attitude that exists there. The attitude – and that is exactly the term used within the culture to refer to this way of being – is an alienated, self-centered, extroverted style of asserting one's social and cultural place. Another Nike spokesman, Charles Barkley, is the perfect example of attitude. Barkley is well known not only for his considerable basketball-playing skill, but for his outbursts of temper: spitting on a young girl sitting at courtside, fighting outside bars, womanizing while away from his wife, elbowing a pitifully mismatched Angolan opponent during the Olympic games, repeatedly cussing his teammates and coaches. It is precisely this part of Barkley's personality – the raging, irresponsible, egomaniacal brute – that Nike (as well as Barkley's other commercial sponsors) exploit to sell shoes. Nike frankly admitted in a *Sports Illustrated* article in 1993 that the company actively pursues attention-getting, bad boy athletes to represent their products.[6]

The athletic shoe commercials represent, commodify, and extend culture. The vast majority of people who admire and identify with Michael Jordan, for instance, have never seen him play basketball in person. But Jordan is not a media creation; he is strategically re-created for commercial purposes. The media make much more of him than he, or anyone, ever could be as a flesh and blood human Being. Every detail is managed to perfection – from the slow-motion, high-flying slam-dunks on TV to the broad, disarming smile staring at us from the Wheaties box. His bigger-than-life media persona is part of an inviting pool of contemporary symbolic resources used to fashion cultural power. The shoes and the competitive advertising campaigns behind them not only turn culture into a commodity, they also extend the culture. But while only industry can sell the shoes, the culture is packaged and sold by a wide range of everyday vendors. These cultural agents range from inner-city black boys whose lifestyle is glorified by the commercial media to suburban white girls who high-five and call each other "homegirls."

The ability to define a situation culturally is the essential proposition of cultural power. This can be done in a restrictive or permissive way. Controlling a decision about which language will be used in a particular context is one fundamental way to define the situation culturally. The fierce debates over the "English only" principle in the United States, for instance, is really a cultural battle. When non-English-speaking first-generation immigrants are required to speak English at school or work, the apprehension they feel is not just about language and communication, but about culture. Even when a language is spoken with perfect clarity and skill, a slight foreign accent can raise questions for some about the speaker's intentions and loyalties. Furthermore, the language/culture relationship is not limited to vocabulary, grammar, and pronounciation. Institutions also try to regulate when people can speak, to whom, about what, and at what volume level. Institutionalized cultural management also shows up, for example, in school dress codes that tell students what clothing and hairstyles are culturally acceptable. These codes are meant not only to standardize appearance and conduct, but to allow authorities to demarcate social power differences between themselves and their culturally unmanageable subjects.[7]

But language, hairstyles, clothes, and virtually all other cultural features can be used in positive, permissive, creative ways too. Such symbolic exploration is basic to how youth communicate and construct culture (Willis, 1990; Lull, 1992a). Young people on the margins of the mainstream are particularly active cultural scavengers and bricoleurs, combing their environments – especially the symbolic arenas – in search of materials with which to assemble their identities and express their beliefs and values as cultural style (Hebdige, 1979). Exercising cultural power frequently means changing social rules away from how people *should* behave to how they *can* behave. This can be the case collectively, as in the uprisings against communist rule and authority, and it is true of oppositional individual activity too. Recall, for instance, the example I gave in chapter 1 about how punks have reconverted the institutional message on a London subway car from "do not obstruct the door" to "obstruct the door." Doing so, the punks not only call for a (symbolic) specific action and assert ideology, but make a cultural statement advocating both a way of thinking and a way of living.

Music is a domain of popular culture where we easily find many clear examples of how cultural power is exercised. Consider, for instance, the cultural dimensions and potentialities of 1950s rock and roll. The 1950s is much more than an era in the history of popular music. It is a widely recognized, distinct, and romanticized cultural space too. Characteristic styles of dress, dance, language, and gender relations are among the cultural features associated with the original rock and roll era. These images will be with us forever. Laser disc, video, film, and kinescope recordings make it possible for the symbolic representations of this and other popular cultures to be preserved forever and put to use by people decades after a cultural moment has completed its original cycle.

For middle-aged baby boomers, invoking cultural style by using 1950s rock and roll music is a way to reclaim one's youth and display cultural competence to others. Doing so temporarily privileges a (partial) way of life – in this case teen rebelliousness, the quest for fun, and feeling sexy. All popular music forms have their specific cultural associations and implications. America's contemporary hip-hop culture – the urban, mainly black youth subculture associated with rap music – reveals a far-reaching use of music for developing cultural identity and influencing society. Taking the place of high-profile media celebrities for many adolescents and young men and women are rap singers and the accoutrements and social relations of hip-hop culture. Rap is a source of information, a point of view, and an attitude. Public Enemy's Chuck D calls rap the "black CNN." The most radical rap artists – the "gangsta rappers" – articulate blatantly oppositional messages and endorse extreme, often violent, cultural values and practices.[8] How rap is heard by a person, however, is greatly influenced by that person's cultural orientation and socioeconomic standing. Rap speaks matter-of-factly to the everyday circumstances of many urban black youth, for instance, while it simultaneously serves the fashion needs and cultural interests of other listeners who live light years away from the inner cities.

If we think of dominant social groups as a cultural major chord, then subcultures are the minor chords – not lesser forms, but playing in a different, often cooler, sexier register. Subcultural groups express themselves through distinctive style such as that we associate with hip-hop, grunge, punk, reggae, and heavy metal, for example. They often form, develop, and ascend with the times politically. This was the case in the hippie era of the 1960s, for instance, when protest music became a major ideological weapon in the political and cultural battles raging at the time. A more recent case is the former East Germany where rock music was a major form of subcultural resistance in the struggle against Erich Honecker's repressive communist regime (Wicke, 1992). In Algeria today political and cultural resistance is expressed in the underground *rai* ("thought" or "will") music. Chinese pop singer Cui Jan was a strong cultural force in the student-worker rebellion there in the late 1980s. The list of examples where music has been used in political and cultural struggle is endless. Because of its accessibility and plasticity, music may be the perfect subcultural medium (Lull, 1992a).

Of course, even the most anarchistic cultural materials and political statements can be packaged and sold for profit. Original rock and roll, acid rock, folk rock, punk, heavy metal, and rap, for instance, have all served the ambitions not only of their originating subcultures, but of the culture industries and people who identify more with mainstream values. Many mainstream trends in fashion, language, and dance began in subcultural forms of expression. All celebrities end up depending in one way or another on agencies of the dominant culture, especially the commercial mass media, to spread their influence – no matter how fierce the message. This was the case of rap singer Ice T's "Cop Killer" song, for example, which, until its eventual removal from the album, made hundreds of thousands of dollars for Warner Communications. The commercial dimensions of popular culture and subculture far surpass the sale of music. Music critic Leonard Pitts Jr of the *Miami Herald*, for instance, points out that "rap fashion has contributed to the surging popularity of sportswear and leisure wear, particularly Chicago White Sox caps, mock team jerseys, and L.A. Raiders jackets. On television, even Fred Flintstone and Barney Rubble have used rap to move boxes of Fruity Pebbles off the shelf. Hammer shills for Taco Bell and Kentucky Fried Chicken; Heavy D peddles Sprite; the Fresh Prince is a Monday night staple on NBC. And you can bet that even Dan Rather knows what a 'homeboy' is." It isn't just the white-owned mainstream media that exploit such subcultural phenomena, either. Black music producer Quincy Jones publishes a slick, advertising-saturated magazine for the hip-hop crossover (read "white suburban") audience, for example, and Spike Lee netted millions with the "X" logo baseball caps, leather jackets, and tee-shirts commemorating the release of his *Malcolm X* movie.

Popular cultural capital: black gold

The mass media, especially television, have been targeted in complaints over the years that they blatantly stereotoype racial groups, particularly African Americans. Certainly to dismiss blacks with the age-old stereotype of "singers, dancers, and athletes" is an incomplete, misleading, and racist evaluation. But such a dismissal also grossly misunderstands the power of popular culture. The strength and gracefulness of the black athlete, the majestic tones of black singers, and the quick, fluid movement of black dance styles are among the most aesthetically appealing and sexually tantalizing forms of contemporary popular culture. Singers, dancers and

Photo 3.2 Transnational popular culture. Malcolm X as a commercial product and cultural resource in Brazil (photo by Vicente de Paulo)

athletes are cultural heroes of the first order. Although the media continue to concentrate on stereotypical aspects of American black (and other) cultures in pursuit of corporate profits by keeping characters and stories predictable, they also single out and glamorize images that many people, especially youth, find extremely attractive.

Ironically, then, the mainly white-owned commercial mass media and culture industries, including sports franchises, are largely responsible for promoting black popular culture to the celebrated status it has attained worldwide. This didn't happen overnight. Black musicians, for instance, were not given recording contracts by the music industry until well into this century. Black athletes were banned from the professional leagues. Black actors rarely found regular work in American television and film until the 1970s. The reluctance to feature black entertainers was eventually overcome when industry realized the extent to which black culture is marketable. To begin with, African Americans are themselves extremely active consumers of pop culture products, especially black pop culture.[9] The technical nature of electronic media resonates sensuously with the oral qualities of black culture. But people of all colors, races, and cultures eagerly buy black music, cheer on black athletes, and regularly tune in black television programs. The market certainly doesn't eradicate racism – some critics claim it only exploits minority races in many ways even more – but it undeniably provides unprecedented access to black cultural space. And this is true not only in the domains of athletics, music, and drama. By the mid 1990s, pop music radio stations in many major American urban markets had been given over almost exclusively to contemporary black musical forms including rap, house, acid jazz, and techno often combined with rhythm and blues, soul, funk, and disco oldies. But just as important, those top-rated stations – whose listeners come from all racial and cultural groups – feature young black male deejays who talk to each other, and to telephone callers, between and over the songs. Listeners can easily drop in on and participate in black culture via FM radio stations. And, after a rough beginning, where black musical groups were largely excluded from the playlists, MTV Music Television and other music video channels have also widely exposed black youth culture. By the early 1990s, and all-rap program (*Yo! MTV Raps*) became the famous music channel's hottest cultural property and highest-rated show. Black veejays routinely engage black artists and fans in conversation on MTV. The nationally syndicated Arsenio Hall television talk show – where black vernacular, subjects, and styles of discussion also dominate – has been another wide avenue to everyday black culture.

The success of black popular culture is by no means limited to developments in the United States or the United Kingdom. And while transnational commercial media and culture industries are largely responsible for the effective spread of black popular culture to most parts of the world, this is not the only vehicle for success. Brazil, like America, has a large black population. The government decided as part of domestic policy in the 1930s to make black culture an important part of national identity. The element of black culture selected to accomplish this task was samba music and dance. The media designated to spread the influence of samba were radio and the record industry (Rowe and Schelling, 1991). This historical development did not help Brazil's black community very much economically, politically, or socially, but it did provide powerful cultural capital for blacks in Brazil, and for all Brazilians as they are perceived by people living outside the huge South American country. As Colombian Jesús Martín-Barbero observed about his neighboring culture: "The black physical gesture became the heart of the popular . . . the passage which started from the *candomble* [an Afro-Brazilian religion] and followed a winding path, twisted and overlaid with other meanings, finally brought music to the record and the radio" (1993: 174).

We can use the case of black popular culture to help illustrate the relationship between race and culture as well. Let me once again use an example from American media. The comedian Sinbad, former host of *Showtime at the Apollo*, a popular late-night weekend TV program originating from the famous theater in Harlem, paid the highest compliment he could one week when he introduced a talent contest entrant as "the blackest white man I ever met!" Every nonblack guest on this lively show must be able to do one thing: be black. They don't have to *be* black, but they must be *black* – American black, that is. Actual black Africans are generally regarded by most black American youth as hopelessly uncool. The racially black audience at the Apollo doesn't mind if white, Asian, or other singers, dancers, or comedians compete by copying black style. In fact, they applaud wildly when it is done successfully. But the point is you better get it right! You better be (American) black *culturally*. Those who are black racially have an inside track on being black culturally. White rap singers more than anyone these days feel pressure to prove they are black enough to perform a style of popular music so clearly associated with black culture. Vanilla Ice's stage name is an aggressive attempt to prove cultural blackness. The Average White Band took the same tack years ago. New Kids on the Block and Marky Mark are still trying to overcome their suburban blandness. Madonna self-consciously courts black fans, and gets them. The black audience wants to know if your soul is for real; if you're white, it probably isn't. The "black power" and "black is beautiful" social movements originating in the 1960s spoke to much more than color, race, and politics. These were cultural primal screams: "Say it Loud! I'm Black and I'm Proud!." Black power is black cultural power, which is now widely appropriated by media institutions of all types and by audiences of all colors and cultures. Rather than consider the spectacular images of popular culture that appear on the mass media as exploitative, therefore, I suggest we look at the issue from another perspective too, taking squarely into account the extraordinary force of cultural power and the cultural and sexual capital it creates.

Culture and rules

Recalling one of the major themes from the previous chapter, rules meld ideology with everyday life by helping organize human experience. The resulting syntheses help compose culture. Rules "encapsulate cultural notions about correct and incorrect ways of doing things" (Collett, 1977: 20). They extend cultural orientations in processes of routine communication (Lull, 1988; 1990) by providing resources for constructing characteristic repertories and strategies of social action. These are all complex and indeterminate social processes. Rules are set, but not in stone. As we know, rules are explicit and implicit codes of conduct we use to make sense, make decisions, and act, sometimes in accord with the prescriptions of institutional rule makers, sometimes not. So, exercising cultural power by defining the cultural situation – even its momentary and fragmentary incarnations – is to set and reset the rules. By constituting and regulating key aspects of social reality, rules authoritatively organize and assert particular ideas and actions while they simultaneously open up possibilities for creative interpretations and appropriations in the social construction of culture.

Cultural power is a key feature of how this social work is done and what its ideological consequences are. As media audiences create popular culture, they repeatedly confront and work with ideological image systems that promote certain values and lifestyles. In this way, structures of authority contained in media imagery are introduced and reinforced. Preferred social rules may even be explicitly proposed within the narratives and symbolic configurations of media content. Such was the case of the famous *Cosby Show*, for instance. Bill Cosby and his writers forthrightly used the program to cultivate specific social attitudes and behaviors. Audiences were invited to think about a whole host of social and moral issues. Central to the project was an effort to link the program's point of view with Cosby's personal authority and the credibility of television as an unmatched communications medium. Personalities from TV, movies, music, sports, and all other popular culture domains similarly influence their fans with structured imagery that is ultimately put to work culturally by people who have a wide range of intentions and operate in countless different situations.

We live not in worlds composed of distinct influences which we experience in serial fashion, but in universes of overlapping, contradictory, shifting, reflexive impulses that constantly require us to sort them out and work with them in order to meaningfully organize and enjoy our lives. We engage complex texts in complex social and cultural contexts. We all have subcultures of the self and the capacity to reinvent the symbolic representations and cultural patterns we encounter. How we merge symbolic resources into our everyday environments in routine communication is social practice that invites analysis from many theoretical points of view. One perspective on such motivated cultural work is that of the "active audience," whom we shall now consider.

4

The Active Audience

So far in this book I have not said much at all about the most common type of mass media research – quantitative analyses of "audience behavior." This is because despite the enormous number of statistically based studies in mass communication carried out during the past 50 years or so, few truly important theoretical insights have been produced. It's no easy matter to quantify human thought and activity or to know precisely how the media influence their audiences. How can we determine the particular impact of mass media compared to other environmental influences when analyzing human consciousness and behavior? Claims made by quantitative researchers about "media effects," therefore, are typically cast in highly equivocal terms. In his classic analysis of media's impact on audiences, for example, Joseph Klapper (1960) concluded that in general the mass media do more to reinforce human behavior than to change it. Wilbur Schramm's often-quoted conclusion first voiced during the early days of mass communication research – that the media influence some people, some of the time, about some things – still best exemplifies the complexities and uncertainties of media effects theory (Schramm et al., 1961).

The first American communication researchers were inspired by a post World War II enthusiasm for the primary methodological techniques of social science – the laboratory experiment and the survey. These researchers were sociologists, psychologists, and political scientists interested in media's broad social effects: mass persuasion, information diffusion, political and consumer behavior, and socialization. The underlying premise of most of the early work was that mass media's symbolic imagery provokes conforming responses from audiences. The relationship between communications technology and human beings was conceptualized in terms of psychological and social-psychological processes focusing mainly on categories of media content and aggregates of audience members. The research findings and implications were based on statistical comparisons of audience groups.

Eventually hopes and fears that electronic media technology and messages overwhelm audiences were substantially qualified. Media influence proved to depend on many contextual factors which are not easily controlled or measured in experimental or survey studies. There is, however, one strong and enduring line of quantitative-based media effects research. This is the considerable number of empirical studies undertaken mainly by American social scientists during the 1960s and early 1970s (but continuing even today) concerning the influence of violent TV programs on children. Analyzing these effects has been the most significant achievement of media audience research that relies on a straightforward cause-and-effect theoretical model and statistical data. This is because the cause or "stimulus" (violent TV shows) and the effect or "response" (aggressive behavior) can be relatively easily isolated and measured in the laboratory when compared to more abstract and complex dimensions of consciousness and behavior.

Only the truly cynical, massively uninformed, or profoundly compromised person could deny that this body of research cumulatively reveals that violent programming helps stir up aggressive behavior. By studying the short-term and long-term consequences of violent TV, social scientists documented just what parents feared all along (National Institute of Mental Health, 1982). Despite the unusually clear experimental and survey research evidence, broadcasters have typically stonewalled the issue or denied culpability. They usually blame parents for not adequately supervising their children's TV viewing. And one commercial TV network, NBC, has steadfastly argued through the years that people simply don't learn anti-social behavior from television.[1]

The TV violence problem dramatically resurfaced as a *cause célèbre* in the mid 1990s when concern about violence in the United States grew to new proportions. Together with easy availability of handguns, disintegration of the family, economic recession, and decay of the inner cities, violent television, which remains a main staple of programming on commercial stations, is now widely regarded by the general public as a big part of the problem. Nonetheless, executives from the media industries continue to be very reluctant to change their basic position. They argue that despite loud complaints from some quarters, the public continues to consume violent imagery at astounding levels. No question: violence is profitable. People's (especially men's) fascination with mediated violence isn't limited to TV shows or action-adventure movies, nor is it confined to the age of electronic media. American print journalism began to prosper when the "penny press" publications began reporting violent crimes and other sensational stories in the early nineteenth century. Social conflict, often with a violent resolution, has been a mainstay of dramatic forms and media including novels, comic books, film, radio, television, and video. Today, many popular video games give players an opportunity not just to watch, but to inflict violence in pursuit of their mediated martial arts fantasies and other action-filled distractions.

Television systems in nations all over the world have been developed with strict limits on the amount and type of violence they can show. American media institutions have uniquely lacked such supervision. But now concern in the United States about violent television (and violent film, rap and heavy metal music) has grown to epic proportions and some industry monitoring has begun. Concern with violence is a big part of the public's critique of mass media, but it is not the only issue. An apocalyptic view of communications technology as an Orwellian big brother is another familiar theme. This nightmarish scenario is sometimes even fed by the media itself. Movies such as *Network*, *Being There*, and *Bob Roberts*, for instance, sensationalize media power over humanity as the main storyline. A quick sampling of critical academic books also reinforces the popular sentiment. Titles such as Herb Schiller's *The Mind Managers*, Stuart Ewen's *Captains of Consciousness*, Neil Postman's *Amusing Ourselves to Death*, and Jerry Mander's *Four Arguments for the Elimination of Television* illustrate the widespread concern. But despite the gloomy descriptions and dire predictions, one glaring contradiction stands out: people everywhere love the mass media, especially television. People in the world's more developed countries watch more and more television every year, buy additional TV sets, augment their sets with video systems, and are now massively upgrading to a new and improved delivery system: interactive, mega-channel capacity, high-definition television (HDTV) – the "information superhighway." Families in less developed countries can't wait to buy their first TV sets and suffer the consequences of life in modern times.

Uses and gratifications

In the midst of the effects studies, critical diatribes, and popular partaking of television and other mass media, a new and important strain of communication theory emerged during the 1970s to greatly influence the international research agenda for years. It challenged the media effects perspective which had dominated empirical research in communication, particularly the North American varieties, since the end of World War II. This departure from the media effects research tradition – which focuses mainly on the negative impact of media – came to be known as the audience "uses and gratifications" perspective. Within this theoretical view, audience members are not thought to be passive receivers or victims of mass media. Proponents of the new perspective straightforwardly claim that people actively *use* the mass media to *gratify* particular, specifiable human *needs*. The new perspective thus provided an important, realistic counterbalance by emphasizing how audience members positively influence their own media experiences. Instead of asking what media do to people, uses and gratifications researchers turned the question around: *what do people do with the media?* (Katz, 1977). This is what the "active audience" means.

But uses and gratifications research was fraught with theoretical and methodological problems too. How people use media to gratify needs are complex and uncertain cognitive and behavioral processes that do not lend themselves well to empirical analysis. What's more, uses and gratifications researchers – like the effects researchers before them – theorize audience activity in behaviorist terms. Adapting quantitatively based methodologies and theories from psychology and sociology, ultimately these researchers also regard audience members essentially as rats in a maze or beans in a jar. Human emotion, cognition, and behavior are once again reduced to statistical data.

On the positive side, however, uses and gratifications theory reflects a healthy tendency also present in some of the very first studies of media audiences. In various ways, several early investigations documented how people willingly engage media to advance their personal and social interests. For example, radio listeners in the 1940s used quiz programs and soap operas to get advice for solving personal problems and for learning social roles generally (Herzog, 1944). Radio listeners quickly employed the medium to establish moods, bracket the day, find companionship, put themselves at ease socially, and be entertained and informed (Mendelsohn, 1964; Suchman, 1942). From the beginning, reading the daily newspaper was a way for adults to participate meaningfully in public life (Berelson, 1949). Families used television programs emanating from the very first black and white sets to entertain visitors and provide group entertainment (McDonagh, 1950) and as a conversational resource, fantasy stimulant, and coin of exchange in peer group interaction (Riley and Riley, 1951). An ethnographic study of Boston's East End Italian population of the 1950s documented how family discussions about TV programs help people define and reinforce gender roles, solve everyday problems, and chastise social institutions (Gans, 1962).

Beginning in the early 1970s, some scholars tried to extend and refine the theoretical trajectories implied by the early media studies. Two basic developments gave birth to what became the uses and gratifications view. First, the involvements people have with mass media were grouped into conceptual categories which led to the creation of typologies of gratifications the media can help produce. Second, attempts were made to explain how people use mass media to gratify their human needs.

Photo 4.1   The active audience at work. Talking back to the TV for personal and social reasons is common and clear evidence that audiences are not "passive receivers" (copyright by Nicole Hollander)

The most important single piece of research and theory along these lines is the work of Denis McQuail and his former associates in England (McQuail et al., 1972). It is worth dwelling on this empirical and theoretical work a bit because it can help us understand and appreciate the thorny issues that were debated during this crucial period in the development of communication theory. The authors took the concept "escape" as their starting point because then, as now, people often said they spend time with media to escape. But escape can be interpreted in many ways. We can regard escape negatively as a flight from reality, procrastination, or avoiding responsibility. But media do not force or cause people to escape. People choose to escape *from* certain situations or mindsets and escape *into* other worlds. They do so for many reasons. McQuail and his colleagues set out to document different kinds of escape and the various motivations that encourage people to escape. The researchers also analyzed the many subtle ways people say they use media to escape. Being able to escape was theorized as a media gratification. Furthermore, these researchers found that various audiences (for example, people from differing social classes) use media differently and for different reasons. What became clear in this work once again is the daunting complexity of audience members' involvements with mass media. The authors finally concluded that in order for social science research to more fully understand what audiences get from the time they spend with mass media, attention must be given to a "diverse range of content appeals, motives, satisfactions, and experiences" (McQuail et al., 1972: 141).

McQuail and his colleagues also developed category systems reflecting the reasons people give for watching television. The first typology deals only with TV quiz programs. By grouping viewers' responses to questions about why they watch these shows, the researchers found that quiz programs help people obtain four main kinds of gratifications: (1) self-rating (assessing one's own knowledge by guessing along with contestants, for instance); (2) a basis for social interaction (family communication, competing with friends, developing conversation); (3) excitement (escaping routines and personal worries, stimulating the self); and (4) educational appeal (projecting and reinforcing educational values). McQuail et al. then proposed a category system to outline more generally the basic gratifications TV viewers get from all kinds of program content. This typology is likewise divided into four parts: (1) diversion (the use of television and other media for escaping routines and problems and for emotional release); (2) personal relationships (social interaction of many kinds and companionship); (3) personal identity (personal reference, reality exploration, value reinforcement); and (4) surveillance (gaining information and developing opinions about public issues, news). This typology helped organize what had been a disparate, unwieldy collection of survey findings into a list of types of personal and social uses of television.

At about the same time, Jay Blumler and Elihu Katz (1974) published a collection of theoretical reviews, essays, critiques, and research papers that further formalized and vitalized the growing uses and gratifications perspective. In this volume, the Swedish sociologist Karl Erik Rosengren (1974) presented what he calls a visualized paradigm of media uses and gratifications. He tried to straighten up the untidiness of uses and gratifications theory by proposing a communications systems model, the type of which was very much in vogue at the time. The model (figure 4.1) was designed to account for the process wherein an individual media audience member, situated in a complex society, uses the media. Echoing the general tendency of uses and gratifications researchers, Rosengren argued that human biological and psychological needs should be the theoretical starting point for the complicated journey toward gratification. According to his model, needs generate perceived problems and suggest solutions which motivate contact with mass media and inspire other forms of social activity which then either successfully or unsuccessfully gratify the need. But as the model indicates, this is not a simple or straightforward process. Rosengren added an abundance of little arrows from boxes representing "society" and "individual characteristics." This was done to show that people engage the media to gratify their needs under the apparent constant influence of strong but conceptually vague external and internal influences which he made no systematic effort to explain.

The functionalist tradition

Because of its robust assumptions that people willingly engage the mass media and benefit from the experience, the uses and gratifications perspective is often associated with the controversial theoretical notion that mass media function positively for society. This relationship between mass communication theory and functionalist sociological theory can be traced to the four-part inventory developed by the American political scientist Harold Laswell in the 1940s. Laswell (1948) claimed that the mass media do four basic things for society: they survey the environment (the news and information function); they correlate a response to this information (the editorial function); they entertain (the diversion function); and they transmit the culture to future generations (the socialization function). In his classic text, *Mass Communication: A Sociological Perspective*, Charles R. Wright smartly made

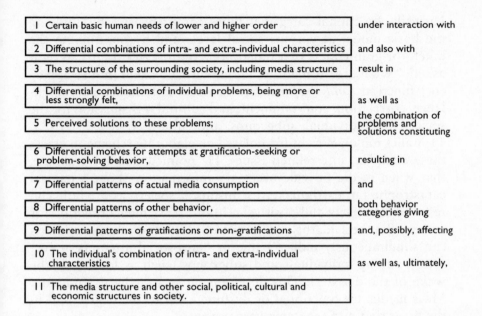

1 Certain basic human needs of lower and higher order	under interaction with
2 Differential combinations of intra- and extra-individual characteristics	and also with
3 The structure of the surrounding society, including media structure	result in
4 Differential combinations of individual problems, being more or less strongly felt,	as well as
5 Perceived solutions to these problems;	the combination of problems and solutions constituting
6 Differential motives for attempts at gratification-seeking or problem-solving behavior,	resulting in
7 Differential patterns of actual media consumption	and
8 Differential patterns of other behavior,	both behavior categories giving
9 Differential patterns of gratifications or non-gratifications	and, possibly, affecting
10 The individual's combination of intra- and extra-individual characteristics	as well as, ultimately,
11 The media structure and other social, political, cultural and economic structures in society.	

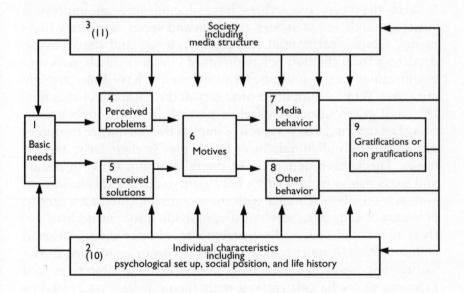

Figure 4.1   Rosengren's visualized paradigm for uses and gratifications research (from Blumler and Katz, 1974)

Laswell's functional categories more comprehensive by applying the basic model at various social levels and by questioning the taken-for-grantedness of a function (Wright, 1960; 1975). Wright asked: "What are the manifest [apparent] and latent [not so apparent] functions *and dysfunctions* of mass communicated surveillance, correlation, entertainment, and cultural transmission for the society, the individual, subgroups, and cultural systems?" (1975: 11; italics mine). Wright formulated an elaborate scheme to assess these complex, interrelated issues. He pointed out, for example, that when media provide necessary information about a natural catastrophe (an earthquake, for instance) society as a whole can respond effectively and positively. In this sense media function for society. But, he said, the very same newscasts and emergency alerts can simultaneously induce panic or "anti-social attempts at survival" among individuals and subgroups (such as looting in the wake of the disaster). This development is a media dysfunction. Mass media are functional or dysfunctional to the degree and in the ways that audience members use them.

Over the years researchers have documented an impressive variety of audience members' personal and social uses of the mass media. Despite substantial empirical evidence, and the welcome departure from the dull behaviorism of effects research, uses and gratifications theory and research nonetheless have been strongly criticized. Why? A simplified summary of the basic criticism is this. Uses and gratifications research is part of the functionalist tradition. The functionalist perspective implies that media are resources put to use by individuals in order to gratify their basic human needs. This conceptualization of the relationship between people and mass media is misleading because it reduces explanations of audience members' contact with mass communicated messages to accounts of simplistic, mechanistic, individualistic, mentalistic activity that is claimed, in the aggregate, to advance the social good (Elliott, 1974). A more telling analysis begins by examining media institutions, sponsors, and messages. When the objectives and practices of media owners and their financial backers are taken into account, it becomes clear that the mass media present an agenda of direct suggestions (for example, commercials) and indirect suggestions (themes in TV programs that help legitimize a particular range of ideologies; see chapter 1) that promote the dominant political/economic/cultural edifice and an underlying system of unequal social relations. Uses and gratifications theory and research only document and concretize this domination when they claim that people are routinely gratified by their experiences with media. In sociological terms, critics say that while audience members may exercise considerable social and cultural power at the interpersonal or "micro" level, they are subject to pervasive constraints at the societal or "macro" level.

A psychological approach

A common and well-founded general criticism of theory and research in psychology is that the study of individual persons usually is not sufficiently grounded in the realities of the social world. Like psychological theories, the uses and gratifications perspective is based largely on cognitive concepts such as needs, motives, and gratifications and has not been much concerned with the overarching, structural issues. Furthermore, while uses and gratifications theorists often try to explain audience activity in psychological terms, they have never developed an appropriate theory of cognition. Despite these problems, a psychological approach to communication can call attention to certain processes and details that are not considered or are glossed over in sociological theories. It can provide partial explanations of audience activity. To study individual persons closely is not necessarily a bad idea.[2]

So, in the next several pages I will follow the basic spirit, logic, and tone of psychology-based uses and gratifications research in order to develop a perspective on certain aspects of human involvement with mass media. It's worth the effort, I believe, to sort out these knotty psychological issues. I will focus squarely on definitive uses and gratifications concepts such as needs and motives and will augment the discussion with other key ideas, including *methods* and the *imagination*. In developing the perspective outlined here, I will draw not only from uses and gratifications theory and research, but also from the stimulating work of British psychologist Rom Harré and his colleagues and what they call the "psychology of action" (Harré et al., 1985). Theorizing the "content of conscious experience," Harré productively synthesizes behavioral routines, conscious awareness, and the "deep structure of the mind and social order" in a critical way that is truly rare in psychology. Such a critical view of the role of the individual in society and culture is perfectly consistent with the argument I am developing in this book.

Needs

Virtually all uses and gratifications theorists recommend using a central psychological concept – need – as the starting point in their analyses. They differ, however, on what they think needs are. Rosengren, for example, defines need as "the biological and psychological infrastructure that forms the basis of all human social behavior" and believes that "a bundle of biological and psychological needs . . . *makes* us act and react" (1974: 270; italics mine). Katz et al. trace the genesis of need to what they vaguely identify as its "social and psychological origins" (1974: 14). McQuail et al. believe that needs come from "social experience" and that even the mass media "may occasionally help to generate in the audience member an awareness of certain needs in relation to his social situation" (1972: 144). In the end, all these writers admit they are at a loss to explain what needs really are. Inevitably, they defer to conceptions of need grounded in psychological theories of motivation such as the self-actualization approach of Abraham Maslow (1954; 1962) or the psychosexual/psychosocial synthesis of Erik Erikson (1982). Because needs are not directly observable, we can only speculate about their origins and forms. It has been useful, therefore, to turn to psychologists for definitions and typologies. And for good reason. Within psychology the concept "need" is the foundation of some of the discipline's most important theoretical work including cognitive dissonance theory, social exchange theory, attribution theory, and some strains of psychoanalytic theory.

The American psychologist Frederick Samuels has reviewed the history of need as a psychological concept. He points out that survival (or physiological) needs such as the requirement for food, water, and sleep are part of every theorist's category system. Furthermore, he notes that even among theorists who "have moved beyond [considering] physiological needs . . . as the bases for human behavior" there is a general consensus that "need is something fundamental to the nature of the human individual. It is resident in that individual, whether or not he is aware of it" (Samuels, 1984: 4). Physiological and psychological needs such as personal safety, social belongingness, and self-esteem may even "lie within the pre-self core of every human being at birth," according to Samuels (p. 203). Other more abstract conceptions of need such as self-actualization, cognitive needs (such as curiosity), aesthetic needs, and expressive needs are less clearly delivered with us at birth, but are nonetheless central to human experience. Furthermore, needs are not independent from one another. Some needs are contained within or overlap other needs.

The very term "need" implies a state of deprivation such as hunger or thirst, or a requirement for essentials such as shelter, personal safety, and basic cognitive and social stability. No doubt these needs are fundamental to the individual's well-being. But gratifying a need can mean much more than responding to biological or psychological deficiencies. Most psychologists believe that human beings are also driven to discover, grow, transcend, and share. These advanced needs are discussed, for example, in Maslow's famous hierarchy of needs. The higher-level needs become salient when biological and safety needs are met.

No matter how essential needs are to people everywhere, they are not universal in form. As Harré et al. argue, "It may even be the case that different cultures, by emphasizing one sort of emotion rather than another, may produce people whose physiological systems differ from one another" (1985: 7). Furthermore, Harré et al. say, "biological imperatives demand that we eat; but cultural imperatives determine the cuisine, our table manners, and the ritual significance with which many meals are taken" (p. 31). Needs are influenced by culture not only in the ways they are formed, but in how they are gratified too. Our need to "belong," for instance, is gratified in terms of experiences and sentiments that surround family, race, ethnicity, gender, religion, social class, and nation (Samuels, 1984: 205). Thus, culturally situated social experience reinforces basic biological and psychological needs while simultaneously giving direction to their sources of gratification. This is a crucial point because it means that we must carefully consider the actual contexts of need gratification. It is here that the mass media enter the picture, and understandings about exactly what needs are, where they originate, and how they are gratified become quite perplexing. Need is a concept that can even be manipulated for profit.

Uses and gratifications theorists have contributed to the confusion by defining need inconsistently in the practice of their research. For instance, while the researchers call for inventories and hierarchies of *psychological* needs, they nonetheless discuss a variety of *"media-related* needs" (Katz et al., 1974: 24). McQuail and his colleagues (1972), for example, discuss a "need" for information, diversion, and social integration. By talking about needs this way, the meaning of the concept shifts away from its biological and psychological origins. From a psychological perspective, a basic need cannot be for information. Instead, it could be a need for personal security, something that information may be perceived to provide. So, a profound theoretical problem in uses and gratifications research crops up with this imprecise use of the central concept "need." If uses and gratifications theory is to be based on a set of causal relations between and among biological/psychological conditions and media-related social practices, we must think of information or entertainment not as something needed by the person, but rather as something *used* to gratify a deep personal requirement or yearning.

Even more important are the ambiguities and controversies surrounding the origins and consequences of human needs. Beyond basic survival requirements, what does the human being truly need? From whose point of view and with what costs and benefits for whom? If some needs are socially constructed, isn't it then the case that people may be told they need things they can do very well without? Questions such as these constitute the classic anti-capitalist critique of needs made by Herbert Marcuse. In his book *One Dimensional Man*, Marcuse argues that market forces try to persuade us to believe in "false needs" which differ from "true needs." False needs are:

> superimposed upon the individual by particular social interests in [the social actor's] repression . . . No matter how much such needs may have become the individual's own, reproduced and

fortified by the conditions of his existence; no matter how much he identifies himself with them and finds himself in their satisfaction, they continue to be what they were from the beginning – products of a society whose dominant interest demands repression. (1964: 5)[3]

It is precisely the confusion about what needs really are that commercial advertisers try to exploit. Even without considering the political polemics that Marcuse's argument inspires, we see again that the concept is not something easily agreed upon. Critical theorists insist that if many needs are learned (or "cultivated;" Giddens, 1991: 170–1), then isn't it essential to identify and analyze the social forces that shape needs? Shouldn't this be the focus of the analysis? In his incisive critique of uses and gratifications theory, Phillip Elliott argued that the active audience member is still primarily a *social* actor subject to ideological and cultural influence:

To reject the idea of an active, purposive audience out of hand would be to adopt a completely determinist view . . . [but] it is necessary to suggest that he orients his behavior toward the external world rather than internal mental states. (1974: 255)

People intentionally engage the social world in order to gratify their needs. These social actions require energy and basic direction, which psychologists generally attribute to *motives*.

Motives

A motive is an impulse or drive that energizes human action along the cognitive/behavioral trajectory toward need gratification. A motive does not have to be consciously perceived. It is more a "feeling state" (Giddens, 1991: 64).[4] A motive is not only a physical drive but a rudimentary cognitive orientation directed toward need gratification. Such energy is not without order. There exists "a dynamic relation between motivation and intentionality" (Giddens, 1984: 13). Thus, whenever we analyze the physical and cognitive actualization of needs (or however we want to conceptualize motivated behavior), we run squarely into questions of politics, economics, ideology, and culture. We must find out where the little arrows in Rosengren's model (figure 4.1) come from and whose interests they represent. When people attempt to gratify their need for love, social acceptance, or belonging, for instance, they are being constantly exposed to suggestions about how to gratify those inner necessities. Motivational impulses are not random. They reflect social experience. There is a dynamic relation, therefore, between inner agitations of the self and the organization of the external world: "What people orient to in everyday life, what they feel is worth discussing, and trying to manage, are their hopes and fears, their dreams, anxieties, guilts, worries, and so on, and the structural properties of the social relations and institutions in which they find themselves enmeshed" (Harré et al., 1985: 29–30). It is exactly this contested emotional space that some information agents – advertisers, for example – try to influence by cultivating "unhappiness . . . fears, anxieties and the sufferings of personal inadequacy" (Bauman, 1989: 189). Commercial solutions are proposed. Need-based, motivated human action thus proceeds toward gratification and other consequences. The direction this process takes for any individual is influenced by contact with a culture's characteristic themes which are mobilized by its primary vehicles of socialization and cultivation – the mass media.

Methods

I no longer feel impelled to go out in the hot sun to play softball with the young bloods at the department picnic. The perceived need to uphold the "macho" image has diminished. Now it should be noted that maintaining a "macho" image is – strictly speaking – not an actual need; it is thus a misperceived need. However, it may be legitimately considered as one possible way, as a *means*, to satisfy an actual basic need – self esteem. In my older age I find other ways than knocking around a horsehide sphere to obtain self esteem. (Samuels, 1984: 18)

In this little story, Frederick Samuels makes the crucial distinction between need and means, or what I call *method*. Let's put it this way: a method is a motivated means for gratifying a need. In the account given above the method is composed of a cognitive plan (maintaining a "macho" image) and an activity (playing softball) all of which is designed to gratify a need (for self-esteem). Methods such as this one may or may not be consciously planned or recognized. They may or may not be successful. They are constantly revised. Furthermore, much human behavior – including contact with the mass media – is *not* motivated by a desire to gratify a need. In the next few pages I will untangle and expand upon these distinctions and give several examples to show how social actors construct methods and use the media for various purposes. I will hold onto the basic assumptions of the psychology-based uses and gratifications perspective in my theoretical elaboration, though this manner of theorizing by no means represents my overall point of view. I will not limit the discussion to an analysis of cognitive operations as if these mental processes occur unaffected by ideology and culture. As I argue throughout this book, analyzing the ways microsocial communication processes interact with social structure should be at the heart of theory. Rules and methods constitute this interaction. Harré and his colleagues succinctly describe the complex intermingling of social forces this way: "[social] action . . . is the product of agents following rules and conventions to realize their intentions, plans, and projects" (1985: 16). By focusing on method, we can keep the delicate synthesis of social structure and social action at the forefront of analysis where it belongs.

These forces are not independent of each other. People devise methods of social and mediated (or "parasocial") interaction in order to achieve various personal and social objectives. They draw from the environment in order to carry out their methods. But while it may be the case that the energy needed to inspire such activity is the social actor's own, the methods used to accomplish these goals are not entirely his or hers. They are suggested by various agents of socialization, especially the commercial mass media. They are also subject to rules: "a person acquires a fragment of the rules and conventions of their society, in accordance with which they form projects for action and choose the means for realizing those projects" (Harré et al., 1985: viii). It is in this nexus of structure and cognition that gratification takes place.

In their attempts to sell commercial products, sponsors of mass-mediated imagery often try to confuse need with method. *Advertisers attempt to create a perception of need in the minds of audience members by suggesting potentially successful methods.* Let me illustrate how this works with a straightforward example from television. For years the primary advertising campaign undertaken by a major Japanese automobile manufacturer featured the slogan "You Need This Car!" This example typifies commercial short-circuiting of the reasoning process. The often-repeated suggestion that the consumer "needs" a product is designed to provoke a genuine feeling that the commodity itself is the need. But in the example given above, for instance, the product (the car) is actually a method, not a need. There are many ways to achieve self-esteem and certainly not all of them are accomplished through material displays. Mother Teresa, who does not drive a luxury car, probably does not lack self-esteem.

The attempt to assert material goods as needs is part of an overall strategy used by advertisers to deliberately confuse and "displace" meaning. The Canadian anthropologist Grant McCracken (1990) offers an interesting perspective on how this works. He says that advertisers market their products in ways that are designed to capture (or recapture) emotional conditions, social circumstances, and lifestyles that have been purposefully displaced and made distant. Commodities are then made available to help the consumer gain (or regain) that which is made to appear out of reach – the golden past, bright future, or alternative present. Consumer goods are promoted as the "objective correlatives" of displaced meaning – "purchases [that can] give the consumer access to displaced ideals" (McCracken, 1990: 116). The frenzy to chase displaced ideals engenders a never-ending search for self-satisfaction. As Anthony Giddens relates, "the project of the self becomes translated into one of the possession of desired goods and the pursuit of artifically-framed styles of life . . . The consumption of ever-novel goods becomes in some part a substitute for the genuine development of the self" (1991: 198). The effect is exponential. As McCracken points out, "from the moment of introduction, the new good begins to demand new companion goods. The individual who assents to the first demand finds that it is followed by a hundred others . . . higher and higher levels of consumption are seen as the loci of pleasure where in fact they are only dulling, boring comfort" (1990: 125, 128).

For purposes of our discussion here, the point is this: mass media endlessly suggest methods for gratification of human needs. Methods are sometimes substituted for needs and meaning is displaced away from the real to the ideal as part of the overall design to constantly promote consumer anxiety and provide a multitude of profitable short-term material solutions. These images may even accumulate to represent particular cultural norms. They are further differentiated by gender. Women are told they need certain things and men other things. But as we know, such cultural representations are not uncritically consumed by audiences. In the end, it is this tension between the ability of mass media to influence thought and activity, and the strong tendency of individuals to use media and symbolic resources for their own purposes, that our theory of media, communication, and culture must accommodate.

Methods and need gratification

Methods are cognitive plans and activities designed and undertaken by social actors (sometimes outside their conscious awareness) to accomplish particular goals that can gratify needs (figure 4.2). For example, if a person feels lonely and wants to socialize, but is shy or inhibited in social situations, he or she might turn to the media for vicarious (parasocial) interaction (Horton and Wohl, 1956) and need fulfillment. The person thus might try

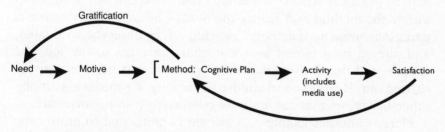

Figure 4.2   Method-satisfaction/need-gratification model

parasocial interaction (a method) in order to gratify a desire for social belonging (the need). When a mass medium is employed for such purposes, this is a "use" of the medium. The use is part of the method.[5] Television is an obvious candidate for such need-based methods. Soap opera stars and talk show hosts receive literally tons of mail from lonely viewers who use certain television shows to interact vicariously.

But the methods don't always work. It is often the case, for instance, that the principal outcome of media activity (for example, degree of perceived social interaction obtained through TV viewing) may not be deemed sufficient by the viewer. This failure may encourage the person to try something else in order to realize the same objective. In uses and gratifications parlance, the person turns to a "functional alternative." This could involve engaging another mass medium or taking part in unmediated social activity. The mass media, people, parties, the telephone, drugs, even sleep are all sources of potential need gratification. So, to watch TV, listen to music, attend a party, or call someone on the phone are all "uses" of one sort or another. Doing any one of these things could certainly gratify one or more needs. The person may try several alternatives before succeeding. So, need gratification occurs in two stages. First, the activity must satisfy the intrinsic requirements of the method. Second, the method (now realized in terms of the activity undertaken) must be able to gratify the need.

To further illustrate the process of need gratification, let me provide some additional examples. A father or mother may determine that one method that could gratify the need to belong is to be perceived by other family members as a good parent. The parent may then construct a variety of everyday activities that could produce this recognition and appreciation. This is a purposeful plan of practical action – a method. Television can be put to use to satisfy the method and gratify the need. Children's TV viewing is parentally influenced activity. Viewing can be observed, evaluated, and altered by a parent in a way that evidences to the self, the spouse, and the children that the parental role is being effectively carried out. Regulation of children's viewing is a media act among other behaviors that can indicate competent role performance.

Here is another example. A person is motivated to gratify the self-esteem need. The cognitive plan fashioned by the person for this purpose is to become an expert on a topic of cultural interest (world affairs, popular music, fashion, etc.). Developing such expertise could qualify the individual as a possessor of important, useful, or otherwise desirable information. Media activities that could be undertaken to achieve this objective include, for instance, subscribing to specialty magazines, reading the newspaper carefully every day, viewing selected TV programs, and so on. To the degree that these media acts successfully facilitate the requirements of the method, we can say that the first level of satisfaction has been reached. The person has become an expert. The adequacy of the method is then cognitively tested against the need to achieve self-esteem. Two types of success or failure can thus occur. The particular activity may or may not develop into a successful enactment of a method. The method itself may or may not then gratify a need.

Human involvement with mass media is not always motivated by the desire to gratify a need or needs. We also use media to satisfy *wants*. Compared to needs, wants are far more of the moment and less central to the well-being of the person. Still, they call out for particular courses of action that often demand immediate satisfaction. For example, a person may flick on the TV for momentary distraction while he or she waits for a friend to call at home. Someone else may pick up a newspaper to glance at the sports results at breakfast. Another person turns on the radio for company while doing housework. In cases such as these, audience members' uses of media cannot really be considered responses to biological or psychological needs. That would be a gross overstatement. These kinds of involvements are motivated by wants. A want is something desired but not needed. The normative environment – both its cultural characteristics and its microsocial expectations – helps shape wants too. The person develops cognitive predispositions influenced in large measure by what society expects and what local environments permit.

Although wants and needs have been discussed separately here, I do not mean to imply that they are mutually exclusive. Nor am I suggesting that they are the only foundations of human activity. Wants and needs should be regarded as points along a continuum representing one perspective on the motivational basis of human activity. Furthermore, although I have specifically discussed television as a resource for need gratification, other media and symbolic forms (music, for example) are also routinely used to gratify needs, although their audiences, contexts, and specific applications often differ from those of television. Because of its pervasive presence and appeal, television (and video) is a frequently used sociocultural resource for constructing need-gratifying methods. The medium's central place in domestic life makes it so unique. Ethnographic research techniques have been productively employed over the years in order to explore the many complex ways that television is used socially. Viewers routinely engage the medium to structure and regulate their environments, facilitate interpersonal communication, gain access to some people and avoid others, learn social behaviors and roles, and demonstrate personal competencies, sometimes with the intention of dominating others (Lull, 1990; figure 4.3). Furthermore, the ways people use television for these purposes differ considerably from one culture to another (Lull, 1988; 1990).

Structural

Environmental: background noise; companionship; entertainment

Regulative: punctuation of time and activity; talk patterns

Relational

Communication facilitation: experience illustration; common ground; conversational entrance; anxiety reduction; agenda for talk; value clarification

Affiliation/avoidance: physical, verbal contact/neglect; family solidarity; family relaxant; conflict reduction; relationship maintenance

Social learning: decision making; behavior modeling; problem solving; value transmission; legitimization; information dissemination; substitute schooling

Competence/dominance: role enactment; role reinforcement; substitute role portrayal; intellectual validation; authority exercise; gatekeeping; argument facilitation

---

Figure 4.3 The social uses of television

Imagination and method

I'll never forget a little conversation I had with a married friend when I was 19 years old. My friend, then in his early 20s, told me he never masturbated. When I asked him why, he said he was afraid of it: "I don't want it to come between my wife and me." What my friend was telling me about is the power of the imagination – the power of the mind to produce vivid images and scenarios.[6] Upon their release from Lebanon and Iran, Western hostages who had been detained for years said only one thing had been left to them in captivity – their imagination. Using it well made survival possible. The dramatic drop in favorable opinion held by voters toward Bill Clinton the weekend before the 1992 American presidential election was blamed by experts on one thing: with such an enormous lead in the polls the week before, many people began to seriously imagine him as president and didn't like what they saw.

In his remarkable book *The Body in the Mind*, Mark Johnson argues for the central place of the imagination in all that we do. For Johnson, whose ideas I will draw upon liberally here, "there can be no meaningful experience without imagination . . . [which is responsible for] all structures and patterns [of bodily experience]" (1987: 151, 139). The imagination, which may seem to be related only to our emotional and artistic impulses, our fantasies, and even to our most illogical thoughts, is also a means by which we conceptualize, structure, and schematize mental representations in perfectly rational ways. It is "absolutely central to human rationality," according to Johnson (p. 168). Thus, the imagination enables us to use our creative potential in service of our rational intentions. This includes the cognitive organizing function: "Imagination is our capacity to organize mental representations (especially percepts, images, and image schemata) into meaningful, coherent unities . . . [Using the] imagination is a pervasive structuring activity" (pp. 140, 168).

One criticism of the media uses and gratifications perspective is that it is too mentalistic (e.g. Elliott, 1974). My concept "method" is subject to the same criticism because it directs attention toward the cognitive and rational (though often subconscious or weakly conscious) construction of social activity, including uses of the mass media. But these cognitive engagements are manifestations of the imagination. People synthesize their perceptions, develop understandings, and determine possible courses of action, including novel schemes, by envisioning what is possible and desirable. Media-related methods are these kinds of imaginative plans.

But the imagination is not an independent, hermeneutic force existing outside social influence. Image structures put to use imaginatively are not unmotivated constructions composed of random images. Johnson fully recognizes that "our ideas and connections do come from somewhere. They come from the imaginative structures that make up our present understanding, from the schemata that organize our experience and serve as the basis for imaginative projections in our network of meanings" (1987: 170). To use the imagination is to simultaneously recall and envision, to symbiotically fuse stock representations (our "present understandings") with creative intentions ("imaginative projections"). Patterns that result are typically influenced by purposive social agents including local role models, work organizations, advertisers, political parties, and so on. The imagination, therefore, is subject to the pervasive structuring ability of the main concept taken up in chapter 2 – social rules. Johnson argues that the "schematizing activity" of the imagination "mediates between images or objects of sensation, on the one hand, and abstract concepts, on the other. It can accomplish this mediation because it can be a rule-following [constitutive rules] or rule-like [regulative rules] activity for creating figure or structure in spatial and temporal representations" (p. 155). Thus, reality is perceived, interpreted, synthesized, and produced through the imagination.

As we know from our discussion of ideology, rules, and culture, people's thoughts and actions are not limited to images, image structures, or symbolic worlds, or to ways of doing things which are already known. Structures of the mind and human action can transcend structures of the symbolic world and conventional behavior into the creative realms of freedom, choice, hope, and the future (DaMatta, 1991: 19). Exercising the imagination is one way this transcendental work is done. It is fundamental to the active audience.

Communication research and cultural studies

Now, I want to place the communication research traditions discussed in this chapter into contemporary perspective. Although quantitative communication (and "mass communication") researchers still produce the greatest amount of published work, especially in the United States, many of the more exciting ideas today come from an academic discipline that originated in England – cultural studies. Furthermore, cultural studies research is typically far more critical than that done within traditional social science. As such, it helps respond to some of the shortcomings of the media effects and uses and gratifications theory and research that were discussed early in this chapter. Cultural studies writers take matters such as race, gender, and social class difference, for example, as starting points in their analyses of communication and culture. Subjectivities and politics are made explicit in cultural studies compared to social scientists' usual claim of objectivity.[7]

Although uses and gratifications research and cultural studies research differ greatly in their theoretical orientations, politics, and methodologies, many of their basic conceptions and traditions are not entirely dissimilar. They begin with some of the same assumptions and arrive at several compatible conclusions.[8] They both focus on audience members' willing and imaginative engagements with mass media form and content. Uses and gratifications research, as I pointed out earlier, developed partly in response to the pessimistic media effects tradition in mass communication theory. The theoretical turn in cultural studies came in response not to the limitations of effects research, which tended to characterize audiences as passive victims of the media, but to the equally misguided idea that media texts impose meaning and influence upon their audiences. Cultural studies essays generally concluded that media texts, because of their content (as it was interpreted by the cultural studies writer), influence audiences in ways that could simply be assumed. It followed, then, that empirical research on audiences need not be undertaken.[9]

One of the key theoretical developments in cultural studies research in recent years has been to show how audience members create their own meanings from media content to control certain aspects of their experiences with media. John Fiske's theoretical work on popular culture (e.g. 1987; 1989; 1993) has been particularly influential. Some qualitative empirical research projects have also contributed to the trend in cultural studies. Ien Ang's (1985) analysis of Dutch women's interpretations and uses of the international TV series *Dallas*, Janice Radway's (1984) account of female empowerment brought about through reading romance novels, and David Morley's studies of family TV viewing practices and the exercise of domestic power in working class London (1980; 1986; 1992), are seminal examples of the expansion of cultural studies analyses into empirical research on audiences. Tamar Liebes's and Elihu Katz's (1990) analysis of ethnic/cultural variation in the decoding of *Dallas* and my own ethnography of Chinese viewers' resistive engagements with television (Lull, 1991) also represent the turn toward qualitative audience research. These studies all document culturally and historically specific ways in which audiences actively interpret and use mass media. Ethnography – where first-hand observations and depth interviewing are utilized to describe and explain communication activity – is emerging now as a very effective methodological approach for contemporary work in cultural and communication studies (see, for example, Jensen and Jankowski, 1991; Lull, 1990).

5
Meaning in Motion

Mass media today reach easily across national and cultural borders, a technological development that directly influences international political relations as it intensifies debates about cultural sovereignty. The impact of global communications has been a major policy focus of the United Nations Educational, Scientific, and Cultural Organization (UNESCO) particularly since the early 1970s. The most common concern is that Western powers, spearheaded by American-owned transnational corporations, have monopolized world communications to such a degree that the economic well-being and cultural identity of less powerful nations have been mightily damaged. The hierarchical "international economic order" and "international information order" are thought to be coactive and complicitous (MacBride, 1980). Some critics consider the domination of worldwide communication channels by technologically sophisticated nations to be modern cultural or media imperialism.

This contemporary transnational, transcultural drama – the "globalization" of material and cultural resources – is, according to Anthony Giddens, an inherent consequence of high modernity (1990: 63). But despite certain universalizing tendencies, the specific forms globalization takes and the types of influence it brings are not all predictable. Nor are they all bad. As we shall see, the monolithic colonizing force implied by the imperialism thesis, while properly critical in orientation and tone, overstates and simplifies what actually happens in specific cultural contexts. A more comprehensive and realistic theory of media, communication, and culture must recognize first of all that ideology-dispensing institutions are *social* institutions not of one mind or voice; nor are the social effects of imagery and technology all predictable. In this chapter we will explore institutional diversity in the mass media and culture industries and the role of technology in social influence. I will further show how media audience members actively interpret and use the symbolic resources at their disposal, focusing on the subject matter this time from a semiotic perspective. We conclude the chapter by analyzing how cultural territories are shifting about in the era of global communication.

Throughout the following discussion, I will again accentuate the ways people creatively and ambitiously negotiate their cultural (including symbolic) worlds. Although I am optimistic about the human spirit and potential, I want to be clear that I have never claimed people act without constraint or always in their best interests. Nor do I doubt for a minute that the privileged economic sector labors overtime to maintain its power. I would likewise never suggest that dominant ideologies are impotent. But staying with a theme developing throughout this book, I will argue that culture ultimately can never be fully managed by any society's political-economic power brokers, including its mass media image makers. Articulations of official or dominant ideologies do not determine culture. Under certain circumstances, dominant ideological expressions can even inspire violent resistance to the power holders. Ideological discontinuities and social disruptions are especially evident in today's fast-paced, contradictory, conflictive world. Although social institutions and information technology clearly serve their managers and backers in certain ways, they can also combine to shake dominant political visions and cultural traditions to the core. This can bring about dire consequences. But before we discuss specific examples of how these complex and dynamic forces interact, let's examine some of the ways industrialization and modernity are thought to influence the production of commodities, information, and entertainment.

Institutions and imperialism

Industrialized capitalist societies produce mass-mediated messages in much the same way they produce commodities. Historical parallels between the two domains of production are striking (figure 5.1).[1] In pre-industrial societies people had to be extremely self-reliant – raising food, constructing and maintaining living spaces, making and repairing clothes, and so on. Because some persons were more skilled at certain tasks than others, pre-industrial specialization, the age of the artisan, emerged. The earliest forms of organized industrial activity, the manufacturing stage, soon followed. Men and women with various talents applied their trade for bosses who managed production, cultivated markets, and sold the first mass-produced goods. Full-blown Western, capitalist industrialization grew rapidly from the manufacturing stage. Assembly lines accelerated the speed and efficiency of production, corporate structures mushroomed, and marketing and advertising developed as essential related industries.

Such frenetic industrial growth, however, brought with it a heavy social price. Workers were forced to unionize to protect their right to health, safety, job security, reasonable working conditions, and a living wage. But labor unions couldn't solve all the social problems that came with industrialization. The overall effect on the human psyche was profound. Anthony Giddens summarizes the classic Marxist and mass society critique of industrialization this way:

> As the forces of production develop, particularly under the aegis of capitalistic production, the individual cedes control of his life cir-

Commodities	Messages
• Self-sufficiency	• Interpersonal communication
• Artisan	• Artist
• Manufacturing	• Independent producer and agent
• Industrialization	• Network

Figure 5.1 Stages of capitalist production

cumstances to the dominating influences of machines and markets. What is originally human becomes alien; human powers are experienced as forces emanating from an objectified social environment. (1991: 191)

A similar historical trajectory can be traced in the production of public information and entertainment. The earliest forms of communication, of course, were unmediated interactions taking place in families, neighborhoods, and communities. But, like the production of commodities, some people became information and entertainment specialists – storytellers, musicians, artists, writers, orators. Development of communications technology in capitalist societies led to the mass production of public messages in much the same way that sophisticated tools and machines, and the profit-driven organization of labor and industrial production behind them, made the expanded manufacture of commodities possible. Public communicators of all types began to depend on business agents and independent producers (to negotiate contracts with publishers or arrange musical or theatrical tours, for instance). Artistic control and integrity eroded as public information and entertainment became institutionalized, commodified, and commercialized.

Production and sale of "popular culture" quickly became a major industry, especially in the United States. This development is represented by the last stage of message production in figure 5.1 – "network," which corresponds to the industrialization of goods. By "network," I mean the complex of culture industries overall, not just the television networks. In the network, information specialists and entertainers lose much control over their work. Business decisions persistently overrule artistic choices in the never-ending quest for financial profit.

Throughout most of the twentieth century the trend in culture industry ownership was toward concentration in the hands of fewer and fewer multinational corporations (Bagdikian, 1988). Furthermore, the culture industries became part of a vast system of interrelated agencies. In the United States, for example, this includes government offices (e.g. Federal Communications Commission, Federal Trade Commission, press secretaries); industry lobbying groups (e.g. American Newspaper Publishing Association, National Association of Broadcasters, Motion Picture Producers and Distributors Association of America, Magazine Publishers Association); national and international information suppliers such as wire services, television program production companies and syndicators, the music industry, and radio and television networks; advertising companies and the clients they represent; as well as individual publishing houses, radio and television stations, and cable outlets. All these agencies have a vested interest in maintaining the political-economic-cultural system. It is today an industrial collectivity and basic ideological mindset with worldwide impact.

Signature trends in today's communication industries began to emerge more than 500 years ago. The origin of modern Western media can be traced to the invention of the first mass communications technology, the manual printing press, in middle fifteenth century Europe. The social implications were dramatic and long lasting. Development of the printing press stimulated a shift in institutional power away from the church, which previously controlled the flow of ideas and information through public channels, to new symbolic and cultural centers and networks (Thompson, 1994). The first major social consequence of modern communications technology, therefore, was to challenge established lines of institutional authority. With the advent of the printing press, "for what may have been the first time in history, a human community willingly harbored a nonreligious agent of social change, and permitted it to transform on a continual and systematic basis virtually every feature of social life" (McCracken, 1990: 29–30).

Further development of communication technology and the shift of symbolic power from one institution to another fostered new ideological priorities. From the very beginning, media industries were "commercial enterprises organized along capitalist lines" (Thompson, 1994: 33). This was true not only of the printing press in late medieval and early modern Europe, but also of film, radio, and television in the United States centuries later. Like their counterparts in England and many European nations, American lawmakers tried at first to ensure that the awesome communicative capabilities of the new electronic media would be used for humanitarian and artistic purposes. Legislation drawn up by United States congressmen in the 1920s, for instance, demanded that the new medium of the day, radio, should not become solely a commercial instrument. But just as marketplace forces subverted social utopian visions in other public spheres in America, expectations of media performance died out too. Just a few decades after the first AM radio station crackled through the airwaves, the fundamental mandate of commercial electronic media – to broadcast as a "public resource" and in the "public interest, convenience, and necessity" – was virtually forgotten. Today, American media regulatory agencies such as the FCC and the FTC are far more likely to represent industry interests than they are to protect citizens' rights. Commissioners are routinely recruited from, and return to, the very industries they are supposed to monitor. The market has replaced government as the regulator of media. Market realities fundamentally determine the international flow of information and entertainment too. Consequently, the more developed nations (the "core" countries) have been able to use modern communications technology to conduct business and represent their economic interests and cultural values worldwide.

For many years, American political economist Herb Schiller has been one of the world's most outspoken and eloquent critics of the grim scenario described above. Schiller originally blamed the imperialist exploits on the domestic and international political-military-industrial ambitions of the United States (1969; 1973; 1976). Schiller claims that while Americans were the first to be trapped in the "corporate-message cocoon . . . what is now happening is the creation and global extension of a near total corporate informational-cultural environment" (1989: 168, 128). And, because the United States still authors most internationally consumed messages, American cultural commodities have "overwhelmed a good part of the world" by "smothering the senses" with a "consumerist virus" (Schiller, 1991). Recognized now more as a corporate than a national force, "American cultural domination . . . [still] sets the boundaries for national discourse" (p. 22).

Communications and information technology, of course, is directly implicated. Worldwide hegemony of corporate ideology, speech, and activity is, according to Schiller and his sympathizers, made possible by communications technology interacting with the "enormous expansion of scientific and technical information, computerization, and the preeminence of the transnational corporation." This further combines with a "marketing ideological atmosphere" steadfastly supported by an American military-industrial partnership in place since the end of World War II (Schiller, 1989: 69, 33–4). Schiller is right that communications technology historically had been developed and used by the military and economic power centers of capitalist societies. Such was the case, for instance, with radio in World War I and television in World War II. Later, allocation of the first satellite channels was supervised by the American-dominated and-housed Communications Satellite (COMSAT) and International Telecommunications Satellite (INTELSAT) which both generously accommodated their first clients – American businesses. From their inception to the present day, satellite channels have been used primarily for transnational corporate communications.

By the mid 1990s advances in communications technology had become truly mindboggling. Again, the immediate benefactors were those who could gain the most materially by an increased capacity to gather, store, manage, and send information. Transnational corporations gobbled up everything from satellite channels, powerful mainframe computers, and multimedia configurations to fax machines, voice mail systems, and car phones. Technology promised to provide a competitive edge for relatively small businesses too. Telemarketers, for instance, used computer-generated voices to make endless sales pitches directly into people's homes, hawking everything from magazine subscriptions to real estate. Capitalizing on communications technology is not just a First World preoccupation. Rich people in poor countries enjoy far greater access to technology too, allowing them to watch international television (via satellite receivers) and video (VCRs), for example, and to conduct business with communication gadgets such as cellular phones and fax machines.

The satellite/cable-television combination became so significant by 1991 that entrepreneur Ted Turner was named *Time* magazine "Man of the Year." The crown jewel of Turner's cable empire, CNN Cable News Network, had turned the human drama and technological glitz and glamour of the Gulf War into one of history's most watched action-adventure serials. Years earlier former US president George Bush admitted that CNN news reports routinely became crucial sources of intelligence that directly influenced his policy decisions, including the official response to China during the 1989 student-worker uprising. CNN's globalizing influence was part of an incredible expansion of commercial telecommunications throughout the world during the 1990s. In Scandinavia and Western Europe, for instance, the treasured commitment to broadcast public service, firmly in place since the introduction of electronic media, gave way to competitive market realities facilitated by satellites. Viewers in the former communist Eastern and Central European nations erected satellite dishes to pull in signals from the West. Public sector television channels all over Latin America were rapidly privatized. The Chinese TV system became more and more commercial every year. And while audience shares for the commercial networks in the United States continued to decline, hundreds of new cable channels now compete for a slice of the still-expanding overall television viewer base.

Institutions and technology: who's running the show?

Let's now question and qualify several assumptions and claims laid out in the preceding pages. So far I have painted a rather depressing picture of institutions: through processes of industrialization and networking, institutions dominate artisans and artists, depersonalize their work, and exploit their labor and creativity. Institutional infrastructure and technology combine to overrepresent the interests of capitalist owners and managers. Using advanced communications technology, transnational businesses monopolize the international flow of information, colonizing helpless Third World cultures along the way. Media audiences all over the world are negatively affected.

Although I firmly believe there is more than a grain of truth to each of these claims, and to their cumulative weight and logic, we cannot leave our analysis at that. We cannot assume, for instance, that industrialization is inherently imprisoning. We must further realize that institutions are not monolithic instruments of political-economic-cultural control. And, communications technology never serves only its institutional creators, developers, and managers. We can begin to make a far more sophisticated assessment of these matters by first questioning the classical critique of capitalist industrialization and modernization, a brief version of which I presented at the beginning of this chapter. Some contemporary commentators believe that the usual critical theories misinterpret history, especially accounts of social power:

> In many pre-modern contexts, individuals (and humanity as a whole) were more powerless than they are in modern settings. People typically lived in smaller groups and communities; but smallness is not the same as power. In many small-group settings individuals were relatively powerless to alter or escape from their surrounding social circumstances. The hold of tradition, for example, was often more or less unchallengeable . . . Pre-modern kinship systems . . . were often quite rigid and offered the individual little scope for independent action. We would be hard pressed to substantiate an overall generalization that, with the coming of modern institutions, most individuals either are (or feel) more powerless than in preceding times. (Giddens, 1991: 192)

Giddens' perspective may reflect a cultural bias in its core assumptions about the desirability of personal freedom and independence, but it does rightfully tear away at a romanticized and misleading account of Western social history. And, today, some long-standing cultural traditions in the East are, in fact, changing. Western individualism has greatly influenced life in Japan, South Korea, Taiwan, Hong Kong, Singapore, even China and Vietnam, for example. In any event, we should not accept at face value the idea that industrialization, modernization, and globalization forcefully destroy cultures against their collective will.

Another assumption of the media/cultural imperialism thesis that should be put to rest is the idea that institutional infrastructure and technology work together in a uniform way to benefit only their owners and managers. Reality proves otherwise. Mass media institutions and technology often do just the opposite; they stimulate ideological and cultural diversity, sometimes precisely by contradicting their owners' and managers' intentions. Although it is true that institutions "may be understood as specific and relatively stable clusters of rules and resources" (Thompson, 1990:

149), these institutions are, after all, *social* institutions. They are social, first of all, in the sense that they are perpetually constituted by human beings. So, just as individual lives and the memberships and agendas of any social group change over time, whatever ideological structures institutions articulate are social inventions which, like their authors and interpreters, are not static. The social construction of reality, then, must be understood as a process that applies as much to the nature of institutions as it does to the dynamics of daily life anywhere else.

An isomorphic relationship develops between institutions and their ideological structures: as institutions change, their structures change too, leading to the further adaptation of institutions, and so on. Beyond this, institutions not only constantly change internally, their positions relative to each other also fluctuate. For example, during China's official modernization period, from 1979 to the present, the overriding characteristic of Chinese society, which at one level may be the most planned and prescriptive nation in the world, is profound disorganization and contradiction within its major institutions and policies – the Communist Party, the political apparatus more broadly, the economic program, the system of jurisprudence, and the culture industries (especially television, but also newspapers, film, and the other mass media).

No single institution can ever articulate but one ideology. Certainly no media institution can. In fact, diversity and contradiction are fundamental themes that emerge when we closely examine what is presented on the mass media throughout the world. This is because institutions all have multiple authors each with their own identities, values, and points of view. The mass media profession often attracts very independent, creative, critical, even rebellious personalities as employees. More than 20 years ago the American sociologist Herbert Gans pointed out that creators of commercial media programming in the United States constantly "fight to express their personal values and tastes . . . and to be free from control by the audience and media executives" (1974: 23). Basing their argument on textual analyses of programs and on interviews conducted with American TV producers and writers, Horace Newcomb and Paul Hirsch support Gans' point. They argue that television is certainly as much a forum for the expression of ideas as it is an ideological weapon of any controlling or dominant political-economic group or class. They claim that the television system as a whole produces a "multiplicity of meanings" and emphasizes "discussion rather than indoctrination . . . contradiction rather than coherence" (1987: 459). Television programs, therefore, ultimately reflect the range of values, beliefs, and opinions held by people who make up the industry.

I spent a good deal of time myself studying television and its audiences in the People's Republic of China before and after the Tiananmen Square standoff in 1989 (Lull, 1991). Although American and Chinese societies differ greatly in many respects, including the ways their mass media institutions operate, I was struck by one inescapable conclusion in my research: despite efforts and pretensions to the contrary, the ideological content of Chinese television is discontinuous and discordant too. Two politically inflammatory domestic network serials, *New Star* and *River Elegy*, were widely recognized inside China as major contributors to the social unrest there in the late 1980s. These serials are only the most extreme examples of the disruptive ideological effects of Chinese television. They reflect strains of an oppositional sentiment that has grown precipitously in China's cities, especially since the middle of the last decade. Alternative cultural and political visions held by media specialists – journalists, TV writers and producers, and film directors, for example – are expressed in Chinese media as an inevitable consequence of multifarious media professionals carrying out their workplace routines. Several factors interact to destroy the omnipotence of any presumed official ideology in China: the diversity of perspectives held by influential workers in the nation's media industries; the inability of the state to manage and control its cultural policy in any consistent or uniform way; contradictory values expressed within the totality of domestic and foreign programs and advertisements; a desire on the part of TV station managers to attract and please large audiences; and the rapidly increasing number of television stations, each with its own requirement to fill airtime. These conditions contributed to an ideological chorus that stimulated a profound cultural reflection and political crisis at the end of the last decade. Even where media institutions are ostensibly used by the official controllers to foster ideological and social unity, diversity and disunity can arise instead.

The social effects of television in China and everywhere else reflect conditions of everyday life experienced by people who work in the media industries and by others who consume media content – audience members. What images appear on television, and how those images are interpreted by viewers, are greatly influenced by the political, economic, and cultural environment. In China by the late 1980s, many urban people – media workers and audience members alike – had found conditions intolerable. Similar developments were taking place in many of the former Soviet bloc nations of Eastern and Central Europe at about the same time. The remarkable thing about all the rebellions against communist authority is that they were made possible in part by the same state-owned and -operated media organizations that were designed to prevent just such ideological disjunctures and social crises. Consider the following events:

- Fearing the political influence of rock music, the former East German government required all pop musicians to follow the strict demands of the state Committee for Entertainment Arts. Designed to shackle the growing East German pop music movement, the policy provided instead a bureaucratic context and location where musicians could meet each other. In these meetings musicians organized resistance to the very government that installed the forum in the first place (Wicke, 1992).
- Despite a yearly budget of less than $100 to buy imported music, the famous East German rock radio station DT-64 still managed to air the latest foreign music during communism's declining years there. Station deejays held clandestine meetings at highway rest stops where their West German friends gave them albums to play.
- An alternative to the official television news source in Hungary, the Black Box Network, forced the government system to become less propagandistic and more objective in its news reporting. The relatively progressive official Hungarian service then influenced viewers in Czechoslovakia and Romania who were able to receive TV signals from their less repressive communist neighbor.
- Liberal professionals inside the print and broadcast journalism industries in Czechoslovakia exercised unprecedented freedom during the crucial weeks leading up to the "Velvet Revolution."
- Romanian dictator Nicolae Ceauşescu cut back TV transmission as part of his austerity program, leading angry viewers to try harder than ever to pick up foreign signals. Videotape trafficking

also increased as even the poorest Romanian families managed to gain access to VCRs. Later, when gun battles raged between revolutionary forces and state soldiers in Bucharest, the fiercest fighting took place at the Romanian National Television facilities. After ruling officials were ousted, the new leader, Ion Iliescu, was sworn into office in the government television studio. Legitimacy of the new government was established by humiliating the captured Ceaușescu and his family on state television.

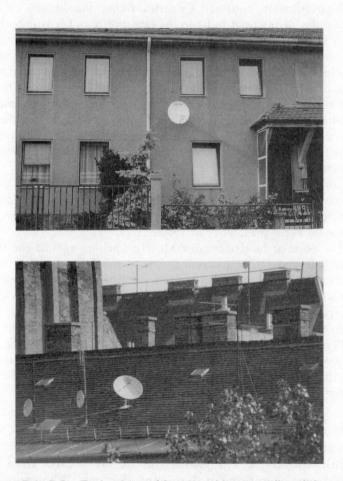

Photos 5.1, 5.2 Technology of freedom. Home satellite dishes pull in ideologies and cultures from outside former communist nations. Photo 5.1: a village in the former East Germany. Photo 5.2: Budapest, Hungary (photos by James Lull)

The resistive power of the mass media is by no means limited to ideological and cultural struggles is communist nations:

- Anti-war protest music by Bob Dylan, Joan Baez, Donovan, and many others was smuggled into the American Armed Forces radio station in Vietnam through private channels during the war. Unmarked music tapes were played regularly during the late hours, circumventing the military's official playlist.
- A government-sponsored TV series, *Ramayana*, became extremely popular throughout India in the late 1980s and is widely thought to have helped bring down the Rajiv Gandhi government. The subversive program stirred up a revival of Hindu fundamentalism which led to widespread political unrest. An Indian scholar reports that rural and poor urban people "created little temples for their TV sets in the corner of their huts. They performed the *puja*, the ritual Hindu washing, before each episode. They treated the series – which emphasized the struggle between 'good Hinduism' and evil – as though god himself was coming through the TV screen" (*San Francisco Chronicle*, April 22, 1991).
- *On These Streets*, a Venezuelan soap opera that weaves political controversies such as government corruption into the storyline, helped stimulate the attempted military coup against the Antonio Carlos Pérez presidency in 1992.
- The popular fundamentalist Muslim uprising against the Shah of Iran in the 1970s succeeded despite the former ruler's iron-fist control of state media organizations. Revolutionary forces spread their influence by word of mouth and the use of audio cassette tapes.
- By the mid 1980s the rock band Los Prisoneros had become one of Peru's most outspoken critics of government actions in the shanty towns. By that time they were also "selling more records than any other group, a mass mediation made possible by the culture industry" (Rowe and Schelling, 1991: 121).

This sampling of situations around the world reveals several important themes. Mass media outlets are multivocal. The impact of subtle subversive symbolism can be far greater than often-repeated representations of dominant ideology. What appears on the mass media sometimes contradicts the ideological articulations of other social institutions. Unofficial, underfinanced media can have greater social impact than official, well-financed channels.

And most important, ideological interpretations and social effects are necessarily, and variously, influenced by context. Social uprisings in China, the states of the former Soviet empire, India, Iran, and Venezuela, for instance, took place because conditions encouraged production of subversive ideology and the construction of resistant interpretations and actions by audiences.

By the same token, when people are generally satisfied with life, and where legitimate avenues of protest and social change exist, even the most inflammatory media programming will not normally stimulate a revolutionary response. During the late 1960s and early 1970s, for instance, Americans of all ages, races, and social classes heard plenty of messages criticizing United States aggression in Vietnam. The music industry cranked out nonstop anti-war anthems. FM "underground" radio stations throughout the country transmitted radical cultural and political messages. Network TV news coverage of the war was depressing and critical. Still, most people continued to believe in "the system." Only those most directly affected – draft-age men, racial minorities, poor people, students, and intellectuals – were likely to speak out.

Defying the power elite: a contemporary case study

Throughout this book I develop and support my theoretical views by analyzing events which take place in real-world cultural contexts. I continue in that mode now by telling a story about an enormously important recent struggle over cultural and political power in Latin America. The setting is Brazil, a country widely known for its robust contradictory impulses – oppressive political authoritarianism and devastating social inequality in the midst of samba, soccer, and the world's most spectacular party, *Carnaval*. Brazil's social institutions, especially the mass media, played an unexpected and focal role in the contemporary political and cultural drama.

In late 1992 former President Fernando Collor de Mello – Brazil's first freely elected president in nearly 30 years – was impeached from office and indicted on 20 counts of racketeering, forging documents, and peddling influence. Collor's impeachment was the final chapter in a fierce political struggle that raged all year. By late afternoon Monday, September 29, Brazil's chamber of congressional deputies voted the president out of office – an absolutely astounding occurrence in such a deeply authoritarian state. The dramatic impeachment vote countdown was carried live from Brasilia on the national television network *TV Globo*. When the deciding vote was cast, people all over Brazil celebrated in a way that rivals only the hysteria of *Carnaval* and soccer championships. People shouted from their apartment windows. Firecrackers exploded everywhere. Automobile drivers laid on their horns. People danced and embraced in the street.[2]

Suddenly democracy seemed to be working in Brazil. What made this political turn of events so extraordinary is that it was brought about by the self-same instruments that had been developed to serve people like Collor – the nation's seemingly unassailable political, economic, and military elite. Without doubt it was the mass media – especially *TV Globo* and the national news magazine *Veja* – that brought the president down by means of their relentless and fearless pursuit of facts related to the mounting controversy. The symbolic impact of impeachment was immeasurable. Collor, the telegenic young politician who won office in 1989 partly by promising to end the corruption plaguing Brazilian politics throughout history, had been unmasked by the very media that helped elect him. This was difficult to believe. Brazilian media have traditionally been viewed in the public mind solely as agents of the masters of deceit who sit atop the nation's political and economic system.[3]

The cultural consequences of Collor's downfall are even more momentous than the short-term political effects. For the first time in Brazilian political history, the people really had their way in the secretive government power games. For the moment at least, Brazil seemed to be a fair and efficient place. The most elevated institutions – the media, the courts, the legislature, and the military – not only permitted but helped create an unprecedented popular challenge to the protected thrones of political-economic authority and social influence.

Brazil's unique institutional authoritarianism can only be understood historically. The nation was granted independence from Portugal in 1822, but political instability, military incursions, and a colonial-plantation mindset slowed industrialization and economic development until well into this century. Feeling threatened by the spread of communism and fascism throughout the world, a group of intellectuals, politicians, and military officers seized control of the national government in 1930. Political leaders joined economic speculators to try to bring about the "order and progress" depicted on the national flag. Brazil's "New State" (*Estado Novo*) was born.

Fundamental to the New State's governing structure was the concept of "corporative interest representation," designed to promote rapid industrialization and provide basic social security for everyone. This would be accomplished by formalizing a partnership between elites and workers. People were asked to trust in the state as provider. Effectiveness of the federal project was to be based on workers' acceptance of the new arrangement.

According to American political scientist Youssef Cohen, who has conducted extensive research in Brazil, the result was a profound paternalism that manipulated people through artificial consensus. The new political structure ended up preventing common people, who had only recently been freed from colonial domination and slavery, from learning democratic values and practices. Instead, the government tried to indoctrinate workers into passive acceptance of their impoverished social condition:

> through the corporative structures . . . Brazilian elites instilled in workers, and maintained among them, the beliefs and values of a frankly authoritarian ideology . . . State elites were thus able to secure . . . the quiescence of workers during the first four decades of industrialization. (Cohen, 1989: 5)

The corporative labor system also insulated workers from alternative courses of collective political-economic action such as labor unions and from diverse sources of public information.

During the same period, from roughly the early 1930s to the mid 1960s, the Brazilian economy and polity descended into grave disarray, Rampant inflation and a declining overall economy, coupled with what people rightly perceived to be a corrupt and inefficient political administration, led to a national crisis. In spring, 1964, a military coup swiftly and a non-violently ousted

President João Goulart. A new brand of authoritarianism was put in place. For the next 20 years Brazil was ruled by military dictatorship.

One immediate priority of the military government was to win popular support, create a greater sense of pan-Brazilian identity, emphasize an urban image, and carry out national economic ambitions in this huge, ethnically diverse nation by developing a countrywide communications system (Straubhaar, 1989; Kottak, 1990). Brazil's television industry, which had developed very slowly prior to the military coup, was the obvious medium to accomplish these objectives. Though Brazilian media are privately owned, the government essentially appropriated the television system and greatly accelerated its growth. The technological modernization was enhanced by a rapid economic upswing (the "Brazilian economic miracle") that took place at the same time – the early 1970s. Within a few years the now world-famous television network based in Rio de Janeiro, *TV Globo*, could be seen by viewers throughout the country. The only other Brazilian national mass medium, news magazines, is read mainly by the educated upper and middle classes.

Although Brazilians throughout the country appreciated being able to watch television, especially the romance serials (*telenovelas*), the medium nonetheless has been widely perceived first and foremost as a propaganda instrument that carries out the agenda of Brazil's military-political-economic elite. *TV Globo's* owner, Roberto Marinho, has himself long been identified as a key player in the inner power circle. Marinho made his position clear: "We are trapped between the political powers, who give us our permit to run the station, and the power of audience opinion. So long as the politicians remain stronger we will continue to support them" (Dunnett, 1990: 195).

So, it is against this agonizing history of institutionalized authoritarianism that the shocking events of 1992 took place. Almost as unbelievable as the eventual removal of a powerful president was the sharply critical, investigative role of *TV Globo* and other media outlets in the democratic process leading up to impeachment. The story, which captivated nearly everyone in Brazil, was popularly known in Brazil as "Collorgate."

The televised uprising of a "passive worker"

A key day in Brazilian political and cultural history is July 5, 1992. On that day, a 28-year-old presidential motor pool driver and former farmer testified before a congressional committee which had just begun investigating possible abuses of power by President Collor. Under heavy guard, Eriberto Freire shocked the committee and the enormous national audience that had tuned in to the televised hearing. He nervously explained how he had been told to deliver various envelopes containing illegal payments on behalf of Collor and his closest crony, a former campaign manager, for deposit in several ghost bank accounts. Freire's stories about illegal deal making in Brazil's shadowy corridors of power were all too familiar to the people. Many Brazilians had hoped that finally, after more than 20 years of military rule, the energetic, young, reform-minded president would follow through on his promise to set the country on a new course by reducing graft and corruption. But Collor turned out to be nothing more than a slick version of all that Brazilians hate about Brazil. Collor was not the solution; he was a cynical prolongation of the problem.[4]

Eriberto Freire, and in their own way *TV Globo* and the national news magazine *Veja*, had become cultural heroes. Freire's testimony was crucial. He spoke out at a time when national polls still indicated nearly two-thirds support for the former president. Freire sat under harsh TV lights, and even harsher questions, to challenge Brazil's intimidating power holders. In Brazil it is almost unthinkable that a menial worker would create problems for any boss, let alone the president. Social class differences, owing to the history I have described, are sometimes manifest in very unpleasant ways. Brazilian power holders' arrogance can be nearly incomprehensible. Imagine this: during the hearings in which Freire testified, and in full view of a nationwide television audience, one government deputy loyal to Collor asked the diminutive chauffeur, "You said you are an honest man. As an honest man, aren't you ashamed to have betrayed your master?" Another pro-Collor deputy tried to disparage Freire by calling him "a poor man." To this, the vehicle driver responded, "Poor, yes, but with the will to work." Freire could easily have accepted huge bribes

Photos 5.3–5.6 TV against the power elite. Photo 5.3: street demonstration in São Paulo demanding ouster of former Brazilian president, Fernando Collor de Melo. Photo 5.4: Carlos Nascimento anchors *TV Globo*'s impeachment coverage. Photo 5.5: Eriberto Freire tells the story of presidential corruption on *TV Globo*. Photo 5.6: Senator Paulo Romano from Minas Gerais casts the deciding impeachment vote telecast live throughout Brazil (visuals reproduced with permission of *TV Globo*, Rio de Janeiro)

not to testify. He also took no money for his congressional testimony or for an interview he gave to *Veja*.

The impact of Freire's story in Brazil was enormous. Many people celebrated the immensely damaging evidence against Collor. But it was Freire's unwillingness to follow the implicit rule to remain loyal to his "master," no matter what the truth or cost, that was even more remarkable. Freire's courageous act was a victory for honesty, decency, and for the poor, who make up more than 70 percent of Brazil's 160 million population. Freire had done the morally right thing. The act was personalized and publicized with nationwide coverage on *TV Globo*. Television had asserted a moral authority that resonated with popular sensibilities and stood in direct conflict with the vested interests of the powerful. The Eriberto Freire testimony, and Brazilian journalism generally during this period, demonstrate clearly and compellingly how, under the right conditions, the mass media can successfully challenge ideological controllers. This is the case even in situations where media institutions appear to be very closely aligned with the centers of political-economic-cultural power.

Can institutions and technology be managed?

State institutions, including the mass media, have been supervised by political authorities in countries such as Brazil and China with hopes for accomplishing specific national objectives. In Brazil, the state wanted to unite vast geographic territories, fight corruption and inefficiency, and keep communism out. In China, the government wanted to unite vast geographic territories, fight corruption and inefficiency, and keep capitalism out! Communication experts in both Brazil and China have also tried to develop and use television to preserve certain cultural values and propagate the structure of authority. But, as we have seen, such intentions can never be so purely articulated or easily carried out. Institutions are inherently noisy. And when conditions are right, as has been the case lately in Brazil, China, and the territories of the former Soviet empire, institutional diversity and ideological variety can burst to the forefront in sensational ways capable of changing the course of history. Institutions and ideology are constantly remade in cultural and historical contexts of social praxis.

This principle does not apply only to the Third World or to the rapidly shrinking communist world. Television can become an unparalleled agent of resistance to authority anywhere when the imagery it presents interacts with troubling local conditions. Consider, for example, what happened after the beating of black motorist Rodney King was televised in the United States. Can it reasonably be argued that repeated showings of this videotape on television helped maintain the hegemony of America's power elite? Or did this highly symbolic event – the white power structure mercilessly beating down a helpless person of color – actually undermine the special interests of the powerful? In effect, the Rodney King video became a one-minute commercial for racial discrimination. The horrific images corresponded perfectly with conditions experienced personally by many disenfranchised Americans, especially poor blacks and Latinos. Later, when the first "not guilty" verdict for police brutality was announced by the media, two news stories – the King beating and the verdict – interacted to spark the South Central Los Angeles riot. Media coverage of the riot then further exacerbated the violence.

What motivated television and the other mass media to pay so much attention to the Rodney King saga? Surely it was the news value of the incident, owing more in journalistic practice to its sensationalism than to any moral responsibility assumed by the profession that produced such a fierce counter-hegemonic barrage of images. News reports of the verdict were played up sensationally too, especially on TV where the King videotape was often shown again. But no one, including journalists or the owners and managers of media properties, could have predicted the startling consequences. The impact ranged from the immediate burning of hundreds of businesses during the riot itself to George Bush's inability later to explain away the problem during his unsuccessful presidential re-election campaign. The Los Angeles riots became a known-in-common political and cultural resource dramatically symbolizing what's "wrong with America." To the degree that the original video, the riots, and the media coverage helped run Bush out of office, American business interests, which are always much more comfortable with a Republican in office, were damaged as well. For those on the other end of the socioeconomic spectrum, one major effect of the King video was to give apparent undeniable credibility to the often-made claim that the American criminal justice system does not treat minorities, especially blacks, fairly. In the public mind, a courtroom conviction of the police officers was not necessary to determine the truth of the situation. The King tape was self-evidently persuasive. In the popular mind, any legal interpretation finding the police not guilty could only be further evidence of blatant racism and a corrupt criminal justice system. The Los Angeles violence was a different kind of vote cast by an angry jury at large.

Worldwide circulation of the Rodney King incident and all that it symbolizes was made possible by a key element of capitalist economic and cultural relations – the market. Television news directors all over the world rushed frantically to put a copy of the tape on the air. Furthermore, the endless showings of the King tape certainly did not require a particularly clever or resistant reading by audiences in order to get the full impact. The evidence was right there in front of all us, displayed and discussed sympathetically by the major media themselves. In this case the power of the market worked far more to inform and inflame relatively powerless people than to deceive or repress them.

The market is what drives the entertainment industry generally in a constant search for the next big money making thing. It's tricky, of course, because culture industry moguls don't want to invest large sums of money in unproven ideas. It's best to come in strong right behind the cutting edge. What is put up for sale must be bought. Then, anything goes. Consider the case of rap music and hip-hop culture. By the early 1990s rap had become an important marketing division in the record business. One of the biggest players in the American entertainment industry, Warner Communications, recorded, packaged, advertised, and sold rapper Ice T's album which contained the song "Cop Killer." The song was widely interpreted as a call to violence against police authority. After enormous sales and a well-milked controversy, Warners rereleased the LP without the song to further exploit the market. Another rap artist, Ice Cube, threatened in the lyrics of one of his songs to "put a bullet" in the temple of his former manager, a "white Jew," Jerry Heller. Ice Cube's album was released because record company executives, many of whom themselves are Jewish, knew it had a viable market – dominant ideology and racism be damned! As Matt Johnson, former singer for the pop music band The The (*sic*), told the New Music Seminar in New York, "The record company doesn't care if you're Buddhist, communist, or capitalist so long as you make money for them." The cultural marketplace ultimately disrupts any pretense of an imposed or unified dominant ideology as manufacturers and consumers of information and entertainment cooperate to produce popular culture.

Just as important as the institutions and markets of the culture industry in creating ideological variety is industrial and consumer communications technology. The 1992 American presidential election was a particularly good example of how technology can enhance the democratic potential. By 1992 more than 60 percent of American homes subscribed to cable television. In many California cities viewers received nearly 100 channels, a number that expanded to more than 500 in some communities by the mid 1990s. Cable channels have given the public much more access to everything, including political candidates. Ross Perot's astounding campaign was launched, cancelled, and reignited on a CNN talk show. Bill Clinton relied on MTV to reach young voters. All three candidates depended on the interactive capability of cable TV and national 1–800 telephone numbers to communicate "personally" with voters. Control over the political campaign agenda exercised by the major commercial TV networks has become a thing of the past.

Just as institutions have diverse lives of their own, technology likewise cannot be completely controlled by individual or corporate design. The Rodney King incident illustrates well how technology does much more than extend and amplify the reach and influence of big media institutions. The Rodney King beating was videotaped by a man learning to use his new VCR. He released the tape to the national television networks who circulated it worldwide. Two vehicles of ideological control – large capitalistic corporations and telecommunications technology – actually combined to circulate an unmistakable, unforgettable, unconscionable image. The result can hardly be considered the imposition of dominant ideology or a technological manifestation of cultural or media imperialism.

Although the global telecommunications industry has realized much of its incredible technological potential, history is full of examples where institutional plans to use communications hardware in specific ways fail miserably or have severe unintended consequences. Satellite-transmitted TV signals, for instance, are routinely appropriated for alternative institutional and personal purposes. As one example, American TV networks and programs, including Spanish-language channels, are intercepted, amplified, and sent through cable television systems making huge profits for entrepreneurs in Mexico and the Caribbean. During the 1989 civil unrest in China, the Chinese government took satellite signals being beamed out of Beijing by Western news organizations, put a completely different narration on the images, and transmitted the revisionist reports back to their own people as part of an impromptu propaganda assault. At the same time, American news agencies were stealing satellite-transmitted national news reports of dissidents being arrested by the communist authorities from the Chinese national television system. The images were then used by American broadcasters to inform and influence their audiences by selectively showing what was happening inside China. By the mid 1990s, some Chinese families had obtained satellite receiver dishes and were regularly watching Rupert Murdoch's Star TV transmissions and other international channels. Government co-ordination and control have been so weak during the economic frenzy of China in the 1990s that the military and the national Ministry of Radio, Film, and Television have even sold satellite receiving equipment to individual consumers, further undermining ideological and cultural control.

The conclusions British sociologist and music critic Simon Frith reached about development of the music industry apply broadly to communication and culture:

> If there's one thing to be learned from twentieth century pop music history, it is that technological innovations have unexpected consequences. The industrialization of music has changed what we do when we play or listen to music . . . but these changes aren't just the result of producers' decisions and control. They also reflect musicians' and consumers' responses. (1992: 69)

To elaborate Frith's point, a familiar texture of 1960s rock music was ear-shattering feedback intentionally produced by guitarists who banged their instruments against high-volume loudspeakers. Years later hip-hop deejays created a radical new sound by rhythmically "scratching" the grooves of vinyl recordings back and forth. Consumers play their part in the mix too. The first phonographs, which were marketed as dictating machines, could not be sold for the intended purpose. Eight-track audio cassette players stalled. Video tape greatly outsold video discs. Audio compact disc players became the industry standard while digital audio tape (DAT) machines never captured buyer interest. Consumer technologies such as car phones, beeper systems, and remote phones, even touch-tone telephones, have been appropriated by drug dealers as sales tools and police alert devices. Home copying of audio and video tapes has significantly reduced profits that were supposed to accrue to the transnational music and film industries.[5] Some consumer technologies in effect ameliorate the effects of the original technology. Television remote control units, for instance, make it easy to mute or avoid commercials. Devices that block out certain TV channels or permit only a preset amount of viewing time are now available. At times the social consequences of communications technology are quite subtle. A woman I know, for instance, saves some of her telephone answering machine messages not for the institutionally intended reason, to preserve information, but to play them back repeatedly for the emotional experience of hearing the voices again and again. Indeed, "technological change is not something that occurs independently of the uses to which [social] agents put technology" (Giddens, 1984: 178).

What we have in modern times, therefore, are dynamic social institutions, including the mass media, that ultimately articulate a wide range of ideas, and ever-changing, expanding communications technologies whose social uses cannot be fully predicted or controlled. This combination produces ideological discourses and technological possibilities which are far more flexible, user-friendly, and democratic than ever before. As institutions grow and technology becomes more accessible, ideology expands and diversifies. User freedom and creativity increase too. Culture is produced not by the culture industries, or by individuals acting in isolation, but in the negotiations and appropriations of publicly circulated symbols. In key respects, technology has helped reduce the gap between cultural authors and interpreters, helping expand and diversify the exercise of cultural power (see chapter 3).[6] Technology works both for and against the interests of institutional power in every kind of political-economic system.

Given all this, any argument that ideology and technology simply smother the senses with an agenda controlled by a corporate master plan does not stand up well to the evidence. There is, first of all, no master plan. As Paul Willis points out about late twentieth century England, the political-economic-cultural power bloc "can hardly agree within itself – as the divisions between patrician Tories, entrepreneurial Thatcherites and social democratic Kinnockites daily demonstrate – never mind imprint its meanings through a commercial cultural sector which is itself seething with anarchy" (1990: 156). We are left to conclude that hegemony ("the process through which dominant ideology is transmitted, consciousness is formed, and social power is exercised;" "dominance and subordination in the field of relations structured by power;" see chapter 1) does not, in the end, sufficiently explain how social power actually materializes. Although every society's elite institutions and leaders find ways to promote their authority by using symbolic forms and other resources at their disposal, no totalizing, controlling, hegemonic effect is ultimately possible. Culture is uncontrollable partly because symbolic representations are always open to multiple interpretations and because ways of living are being constantly reconstructed and redefined.

Making meaning

Madonna not only made it very, very big in the realm of popular culture during the past decade, she became a celebrated and controversial personality in academic circles too. College courses analyze the Madonna phenomenon. Scientific journals display statistical data about her. Scholarly books debate her psycho-socio-cultural-sexual significance. What fascinates intellectuals of all stripes about Madonna are the reasons for her success. Who adores Madonna? Why? What difference does it make?

What we discover right away trying to answer these questions is that many different kinds of people appreciate Madonna for many different reasons. Madonna has zealous fans who are young and old, straight and gay, educated and unschooled, First and Third World, black, white, brown, and yellow, and of every sexual preference, demographic category, and lifestyle imaginable. People who differ from one another in every way can all still find something relevant in Madonna's multidimensional, multimediated public imagery. From the feminist who identifies with Madonna's in-your-face "I take the world on my own terms" attitude to the voyeuristic young male charmed by the "Boy Toy" and "Girlie Show" side of her public persona, Madonna resonates widely with multiple, often contradictory, cultural values and lifestyles, personal identities and fantasies.

Madonna has clicked. Her strong personality, ambitiousness, extremism, and numerous talents together with highly financed and well-orchestrated worldwide marketing have made fantastic success possible. But Madonna's fame and fortune do not result from any inherent personal characteristics. Nor can her achievements be attributed mainly to a media blitz, no matter how expensive. Madonna's success comes from the widespread acceptance she receives from her multiple fan base. Madonna is the queen of *polysemy* (many meanings), and the more polysemic (or open-ended) the text, the greater the popular potential. Madonna is unique first because she strikes so many different responsive chords, and second because the semiotic trajectories and cultural activities she ignites are so intense. What Madonna means is discovered, reinforced, and transcended in the various ways her fans enthusiastically put her to work culturally (Schwichtenberg, 1993; see also the discussion of cultural power in chapter 3). This kind of large-scale semiotic and cultural activity is what John Fiske (1989) calls "production of the popular." People choose, combine, and circulate media representations and other cultural forms in their everyday communicative interactions and in doing so produce meaning and popularity. Thus the special significance and degree of acceptance that Madonna or any other cultural resource receives ultimately is produced by fans, not stars.

In celebrating the capacity of people to use and abuse cultural media and materials for their own purposes, Fiske argues that "pleasure" derives from acts of meaning construction (1987;

Photo 5.7 Madonna – queen of polysemy (photo by Herb Ritts, reprinted with permission of Warner Bros Records)

1989). The pleasure is one of resistance. According to Fiske, people constantly fight back against the repressive, tranquilizing "mass culture," "dominant ideology," and other institutional "forces of dominance" that confront them. Popular interpretations and uses of Madonna and all cultural symbols are "tactics by which the [dominant] forces are coped with, evaded, or resisted" (1989: 20). Everyday life for common people "is a series of tactical maneuvers against the strategy of the colonizing forces" (p. 161). Media consumers are "the people" who struggle against the "power bloc" (p. 163). If such an assessment sounds remarkably like Herbert Schiller's cultural imperialism thesis, there is one major difference. Fiske disagrees with Schiller's certainty that ordinary people don't win their encounters with colonizers from the dominant culture. For Fiske, struggles over meaning are struggles over social power. He argues that in behavior ranging from youth tearing holes in their jeans to Australian aboriginals cheering on the American Indians in their shootouts with white cowboys on imported TV westerns, people everywhere routinely and heroically score victories in ongoing semantic and cultural guerrilla warfare. Fiske's confidence that media audiences do indeed successfully subvert the forces of ideological and cultural control has brought his work lots of attention. He has certainly helped dispel the idea that media audience members are passive consumers or victims.[7]

Polysemy and selectivity

Brahma: to Spaniards, a bull; to Brazilians, a beer; to Americans, a recreational road vehicle; to Indians, god.

Polysemy in particular and semiotics in general have become very important study areas in the communication discipline, thanks in no small measure to John Fiske's fresh theories and stimulating writing. But analyses of how symbolic imagery is variously interpreted and used long predates the recent trend. The early work on these subjects was done mainly by American social psychologists and sociologists. In a classic study (Cooper and Jahoda, 1947), researchers found that a cartoon series designed to reduce racial prejudice ("Mr Bigot") actually did more to reinforce than diminish it. Years later other researchers observed the same effect with the famous American television series, *All in the Family* (Vidmar and Rokeach, 1974). The series's executive producer, Norman Lear, tried to make the lead character, Archie Bunker, look like a bigoted fool. Lear reasoned that prejudiced viewers would recognize themselves in Archie's doltish antics and would change their ways as a result. *All in the Family* became enormously popular and it did stir controversy. But just like the "Mr Bigot" cartoon strip, it did something the producer had not anticipated. Instead of being repulsed by Archie, TV viewers with predispositions like his found him likeable, even heroic. They perceived him to be down-to-earth, honest, hardworking, and kind. On the other hand, viewers opposed to Archie's values thought he was bigoted, loud, rigid, domineering, and mistreating of his TV wife. How Mr Bigot and Archie Bunker were interpreted was framed by readers' and viewers' values and orientations. These predispositions cannot easily be altered.[8]

Another early study analyzed how students from two American colleges interpreted a film of a football game played between the schools. Accounts of the game varied wildly. The researchers concluded that "the 'game' was actually many different games and each version of the events was just as 'real' to a particular person as other versions were to other people" (Hastorf and Cantril, 1954: 134). They explained that "there is no such thing as a 'game' existing 'out there' in its own right which people merely 'observe.' The game exists for a person and is experienced by him only in so far as certain happenings have significance in terms of his purpose" (p. 133).

These early studies in social psychology and communication reveal two fundamental principles that are now being addressed from a different perspective in semiotic analysis and cultural studies research: nothing is interpreted neutrally, and meaning cannot be imposed. It's clear from either perspective that people interpret and use cultural phenomena such as pop music stars, television programs, and sporting games in ways they find reinforcing, stimulating, or otherwise rewarding. Popular culture is not an independent force that works against the will of a person or a society. It originates in and resonates with society at large. When the media and popular culture contribute to social change, this occurs because represented ideas appeal to predispositions and intentions people already hold. The media primarily provide examples and give specific suggestions (Gans, 1974: 57).[9]

Interpretative systems of meaning

When I say no, I mean maybe;
Or maybe I mean yes.
(Holly Dunn, "Maybe I Mean Yes")

You can be anything you want;
Every color you are.
(David Sylvian, "Every Color You Are")

Selectivity and polysemy are not just about interpretations of the symbolic environment. Meaning is not something assigned only to external objects. Interpretative work is also a process of self-discovery and understanding. Every interpretation of a sign is simultaneously an interpretation and transformation of the imagined self. The teenage girl who thinks about Madonna, for example, at the same time takes stock of herself. When a young man in Moscow tries on a pair of jeans for the first time, he conjures up an image of America and of himself too – perhaps of himself in America! Chinese viewers of imported Japanese TV soap operas interpret their own situations along with the stories. All semiotic activity is made up of complex associations that flow back and forth between external and internal worlds.

Such subjective involvements and relationships constitute profoundly dense and dynamic processes of meaning construction. Meaning is never self-evident. Making sense is a full-time job; what Paul Willis (1990) calls "necessary symbolic work." It is difficult in the first place to imagine anything that is not open to varying interpretations and uses. Symbols can mean different things to different people, and different things to the same person as well. Different aspects of an image or text can likewise mean different things to the same person or to different people. A text can be variously interpreted by the same person at different times or under different circumstances.[10] Meaning is compartmentalized and relativized. For example, poor Brazilian women eagerly step through the emotional minefields of soap operas featuring upper class settings and stories, focusing on the emotional realism and social usefulness of these extremely popular shows (Tufte, 1992). Ien Ang's (1985) analysis of Dutch women's subjective involvements with the American TV serial *Dallas* concludes along the same lines. People's varying intentions come directly into play as they encounter cultural materials. Meaning construction is thus creative, expansive, and highly subjective. Meaning is multiple and variable. Symbolic representations are *multisemic* as well as polysemic.[11]

New cultural territories

- Many New Yorkers born in the Dominican Republic regularly return to the Caribbean island nation to vote in national elections and say they consider themselves as much Dominican as American.
- Jamaican reggae music by Bob Marley, Peter Tosh, and Black Uhuru pulsates at high volume in clothing boutiques located in the *medinas* (people's markets) of Fez, Morocco.
- *USA Today*, the satellite-transmitted newspaper published on every continent, now operates Sky Radio whose only market is people aloft in airplanes over the United States.
- More than 400 million people worldwide, in countries including Russia, Tunisia, Zimbabwe, and Switzerland, regularly watch TV soap operas that originate in Spanish-language nations.
- German pop music bands travel to the United States where they perform solely for Vietnamese-American immigrants who use the music to unite their community.
- The radio station with the highest Arbitron audience share in Los Angeles broadcasts only in Spanish and features *banda* music – regional Mexican folk music blended with traditional Bavarian rhythms and instruments including the tuba.
- Brazilian religious cults incorporate dieties and mythologies of African nations with Catholic saints and Amerindian spirits (Rowe and Schelling, 1991).
- The police department in Santa Barbara, California, patrols the Latino section of town in a police car customized with air-brushed door panel murals, metallic sparkle, and magnesium wheels to resemble the "low-rider" vehicles young Latino men drive.

These developments reveal some of the ways cultural territories diversify and expand in a world where people and images move about at breakneck speed. In truth cultural traditions have never been motionless; they are always reinvented by subsequent generations (Giddens, 1990). But the cultural environments we live in today are changing in unprecedented ways and in greater measure than ever before. Immigration, urbanization, and technology all fuel the turmoil. Cultural categories, contexts, assumptions, allegiances, and relevancies are all shifting madly about. World cultures are being continuously recontextualized into new provinces of meaning.

The seeming chaos of cultural change has been described as the "postmodern condition" (Harvey, 1989). Postmodernist theorists typically argue that today's rapid-fire cultural realignments are producing a global society lacking in structure and order. Now that we have satisfied the quest for material comforts and conveniences, our collective purpose in life is less clear. We live in an overly stimulated, yet unfulfilling society. From social relationships to music and architecture, nothing makes sense anymore. We are swimming aimlessly about in modernity's meaningless wake – postmodernity.

I do not want to enter into a lengthy debate or critique of postmodernism. But two comments must be made. First, postmodernist theory is elitist. Most of the world is not yet modern, much less postmodern. Postmodernist discussions typically agonize over the plight of societies, or social groups within societies, who can afford to luxuriate in modern problems. Of course modernity in the more developed world does affect people everywhere, at least indirectly. But to understand how people really live outside places like Europe, the United States, and Japan, postmodernist theories are inappropriate and inadequate. Second, because postmodernist theories emphasize the disconnectedness of signs from their referents, and try to describe the disorderliness of contemporary cultural formations, the sources, styles, and consequences of social power become less clear and are often ignored. Cultural fetishism and the lack of political accountability thus characterize much postmodernist theorizing. Because of problems like these, postmodernist discussions contribute little to social theory. As Giddens puts it, "Postmodernism, if it means anything, is best kept to refer to styles or movements within literature, painting, the plastic arts, and architecture. It concerns aspects of aesthetic reflection upon the nature of modernity" (1990: 45). Furthermore, much of the world's most serious and perplexing confusions, like the ethnic and religious wars raging in India and the former Yugoslavia, have much more to do with ideologies and cultural traditions deeply rooted in the past than with any collective cultural neurosis brought on by an inability to deal with life after modernity.

Rather than dwell on the directionlessness and despair of life in postmodern times for people fortunate enough to live with such problems, I prefer to concentrate on more concrete developments by emphasizing how people interpret their changing worlds, make them meaningful, and advance their personal, social, and cultural interests. To systematically rethink culture this way, I will discuss several key analytical concepts. We will consider, first of all, what the trajectories and patterns of contemporary cultural reconfiguration mean for global cultural developments. We will then explore how cultures and peoples break away from their origins in processes of *deterritorialization* and re-form via *reterritorialization*. These activities involve three related phenomena: *transculturation*, *indigenization*, and *hybridization*.

Globalization

The term "globalization" has been coined to describe the scope of current developments in communication and culture (Featherstone, 1990). But this term must be qualified. We do not live in a global village where a mythic, all-encompassing, technology-based super society replaces outdated and unwanted local social systems and cultures. Despite technology's awesome reach, we have not, and will not, become one people. It is true that potent homogenizing forces including military weaponry, advertising techniques, dominant languages, media formats, and fashion trends undeniably affect consciousness and culture in virtually every corner of the world. Such spheres of influence introduce and reinforce certain standardizing values and practices. But these political-economic-cultural influences do not enter cultural contexts uniformly. They always interact with diverse local conditions. Put into practice on a global scale, homogenizing cultural forces encounter a wide variety of ideologies and traditions producing a range of "heterogeneous dialogues" (Appadurai, 1990). Just as TV programs, films, and popular music don't turn individual consumers into passive dupes in any single society, the power to transmit information worldwide likewise does not stimulate automatic imitation or conformity at the national or cultural level.

Forces of modernity have no doubt changed the face of world cultures and altered political-economic relationships too. But the resulting pervasive globalization is "more an organization of diversity than a replication of uniformity" (Hannerz, 1990). Local and regional influences do not disappear in the face of imported cultures. The very concept of culture presumes difference. As British sociologist Anthony D. Smith points out:

> If by "culture" is meant a collective mode of life, or a repertoire of beliefs, styles, values, and symbols, then we can only speak of cultures, never just culture; for a collective mode of life, or a repertoire of beliefs, etc., presupposes different modes and repertoires in a universe of modes and repertoires. Hence, the idea of a "global culture" is a practical impossibility. (1990: 171)

Even the nation-state, which by some accounts these days is declining in power as a necessary social structure, still demarcates important cultural differences. One need look no further than the effort to bring the "European Community" together to see how difficult it is to unify and politicize cultural differences.

The American anthropologist Arjun Appadurai, whose work I draw upon extensively here, believes that cultural heterogenization (the idea that culture always takes many forms) is much more valid than any theory of encroaching cultural sameness. Appadurai argues that claims of creeping global homogenization invariably

> subspeciate into either an argument about Americanization, or an argument about commoditization, and very often these two arguments are very closely linked. What these arguments fail to consider is that at least as rapidly as forces from the various metropolises are brought into new societies, they tend to become indigenized in one way or another: this is true of music and housing styles as much as it is true of science and terrorism, spectacles and constitutions. (1990: 295)

Culture thus oscillates dialectically between forces of permanence and change, of tradition and innovation. How people organize these cultural stresses is key to understanding modern social stability.

Appadurai specifies five factors he thinks form the dynamics of contemporary cultural diversity. He calls these dimensions "scapes." Appadurai argues that the five scapes assure that cultural homogeneity and domination are not possible. The dimensions of global culture are ethnoscapes, technoscapes, finanscapes, mediascapes, and ideoscapes. Each concept refers to a type of movement. Ethnoscape, for example, denotes the flow of people from one part of the world to another. This includes tourists, immigrants, refugees, exiles, guestworkers, and so on. Technoscape describes the transporting of industrial technology across national borders. India, China, Russia, and Japan, for instance, have all exported technology to Libya in order to construct a huge steel complex there. Finanscape refers to patterns of global money transfer. Foreign investments channeled through the World Bank for energy and transportation development projects in Brazil are examples of this. Rather than advance only the interests of the world's political-economic-cultural superpowers, Appadurai argues that relationships between and among ethnoscapes, technoscapes, and finanscapes are "deeply disjunctive and profoundly unpredictable, since each of these landscapes is subject to its own constraints and incentives . . . [and] each acts as a constraint and a parameter for movements of the other" (p. 298).

Added to these disjunctive factors are two more interrelated concepts – mediascape and ideoscape. Mediascape refers to mechanical and electronic mass media hardware and the images they produce. Viewers use these images to construct cultural "narratives of the other." For example, by portraying African culture on European television, the medium supplies symbolic resources which invite people to imagine life on the southern continent. The last factor, ideoscape, also refers to images, but specifically to the political aspects – the straightforwardly ideological contours of culture. Ideoscapes represent partisan positions in struggles over power and the allocation of resources in a political state. The articulation and dissemination of ideologies are always modified by context. Thus, ideological domains such as rights, freedom, responsibility, equality, discipline, democracy, and so on make up ideoscapes of differing significance in Cuba, the United States, South Africa, Peru, Norway, and Iran, for example.

To repeat the central argument, Appadurai claims that the five scapes influence culture not by their hegemonic interaction, global diffusion, and uniform effect, but by their differences, contradictions, and counter-tendencies – their "disjunctures." Communications technology is fundamental to the argument. The mass media do much more to expand cultural diversity than standardize it. So, "people, machines, money, images, and ideas follow increasingly non-isomorphic paths" in the construction of contemporary global culture (p. 301). Globalization is best considered a complex set of interacting and often countervailing human, material, and symbolic flows that lead to diverse, heterogeneous cultural positionings and practices which persistently and variously modify established vectors of social, political, and cultural power. As Martín-Barbero puts it, "the steady predictable tempo of homogenizing development is upset by the counter-tempo of profound differences and cultural discontinuities" (1993: 149).

Cultural territory is a very important issue for Third World scholars. None of them has argued more convincingly and elegantly during the past decade than the Mexican anthropologist Néstor García Canclini (1989).[12] From the outset García Canclini joins with other contemporary thinkers who no longer find satisfying the argument that political-economic-cultural realities are dominated and manipulated by "large metropolitan consortia." Consistent with our earlier discussion of institutional diversity, García Canclini points out that theories of cultural imperialism do not account for the ways ideological and cultural imagery is created and distributed by the centers of production. It also ignores the multipolarity of social initiatives and the plurality of cultural reference points. The subjectivity and creative unruliness of the arts, mass media, and cultural production prevent cultural homogenization and manipulation: "The aspirations of artists, journalists, and all types of cultural workers to function as a mediator between symbolic camps and in relations between and among diverse groups contradicts the motion of the market toward concentration and monopolization" (p. 344).

Deterritorialization

The first step in the formation of new cultural territories is deterritorialization. This concept, in García Canclini's words, refers to "the loss of the 'natural' relation between culture with geographic and social territory [including] relocalizations of new and old forms of symbolic production" (1989: 288). Two other scholars of Latin American culture, William Rowe and Vivian Schelling, call it "the release of cultural signs from fixed locations in space and time" (1991: 231). Deterritorialization is the (partial) disintegration of human and symbolic constellations and patterns. It is the tearing apart of cultural structures, relationships, settings, and representations. Deterritorialization is a consequence of the cultural disjunctures we have just discussed. It is one indication of the cultural change that the disjunctures stimulate.

The rapid migration of Third World peoples into more developed countries is one spectacular example of deterritorialization – a social uprooting that necessitates major cultural disruptions and adaptations. In this case, deterritorialization is a consequence of the demand for a labor pool to do undesirable, menial labor in wealthy societies. This was true of the African and Asian slave trade in colonial North America, Brazil, and the Caribbean centuries ago and it is also true of illegal immigrant Mexican farmworker employment in the United States today, among many other examples. In cases such as these, economic incentives are at the heart of the social and cultural migrations. The consequences of immigration in today's environment can be severe. The United Nations Population Fund calls contemporary immigration the "human crisis of our age" because poverty, wars, and overcrowding force people to push into territories already occupied by others. The violence suffered by Turkish workers in Germany during the 1990s, for example, reflects how cultural transitions – demarcated in this case by race, ethnicity, religion, and social class – can negatively affect both immigrants and hosts.

Cultural deterritorialization, therefore, is a profoundly human matter. The concept "ought not to be reduced to the movement of ideas or cultural codes," as typical postmodernist discussions might do, but should focus squarely on social, economic, and political problems and competitions (García Canclini, 1989: 305). The prototypical case is slavery. In forced human migrations, deterritorialization can be totalizing and horrible. Taking away a group's language, social customs, religion, and music – as was done to African slaves in the American colonies – is tantamount to cultural assassination. But culture never dies, even in conditions of orchestrated repression. It adapts and survives in mutated forms. Furthermore, the effect of cultural dislocations is never limited only to those who are forced to move. For example, migrant Turkish guestworkers in Germany have an ethnic/cultural relation with the Germans, with each other in Germany, and with the Turkish homeland. All three cultural zones are negotiated simultaneously. Modern communications technology plays a key role in all the negotiations: how Turks learn about Germans (and, to a lesser degree, how Germans learn about Turks); how Turks maintain and nurture their identities as Turks in Germany; and how Turks maintain contact with their culture and people in Turkey. This situation, of course, is not peculiar to Turkish people in Germany. Similar circumstances develop wherever migrant populations congregate. Roger Wallis and I have analyzed how political refugees from Vietnam have adapted to their new cultural territory in California, for instance (Lull and Wallis, 1992). The effects of cultural dislocation and mixing never stop, but they change course. For example today, centuries after the beginning of the slave trade, and with a boost from business incentives and the technological capabilities of modern mass media, African Americans strongly influence cultures of the former colonial powers who imported and enslaved them (see chapter 3). In other cases, cultural reference points can be interpreted in a very selective and creative manner. For instance, regardless of where he was born, where he lives and works, what language he speaks, or who he is supposed to portray, Robert De Niro will forever be an Italian in Italy.

One common byproduct of widespread cultural dislocation caused by immigration is political extremism involving the homeland. Vietnamese in California have mounted a tenacious clandestine effort to overthrow the communist government in Vietnam, for example. Such reactionary activity is not unusual for peoples forced to flee their homelands: "Deterritorialization . . . sometimes creates exaggerated and intensified senses of criticism or attachment to politics in the home-state. Deterritorialization, whether of Hindus, Sikhs, Palestinians or Ukranians, is now at the core of a variety of global fundamentalisms, including Islamic and Hindu fundamentalism" (Appadurai, 1990: 301). The African American repatriation movement of the early twentieth century and later black Muslim political activity are other examples of this tendency.

Cultural melding and mediation

Immigrants cross the city in many directions and install, precisely in the crossings, their baroque places of regional sweets and contraband radios, their curative herbs and videocassettes. (García Canclini, 1989: 16)

When Angolans relocate in Brazil, Turks in Germany, Koreans in Japan, Vietnamese in the United States, and Jamaicans in England, for example, they certainly don't keep strictly to themselves – especially not the young adults and children. In one way or another deterritorialized peoples mix in with their new surroundings. What results is a kind of cultural give-and-take. These cultural interactions are variously termed transculturation, indigenization, and hybridization. Each concept emphasizes a different aspect of cultural melding and mediation.

Transculturation refers to a process in which cultural forms literally move through time and space where they interact with other cultural forms, influence each other, and produce new forms. As we have seen, these cultural syntheses often result from the physical movement of peoples from one geographic location to another. But many cultural crossings are made possible by the mass media and culture industries. Modern technology reconstructs the essential axes of cultural distance – space and time. This is the case most obviously in terms of physical space. We have already discussed at length how the transmission and reception of information and entertainment from one part of the world to another inspire new cultural syntheses. But communications technology also constructs new perceptions and uses of cultural time. Film, still photography, kinescope, audio tape, video tape, and today's digital audio and video information storage and retrieval systems give ready access to cultural histories. The electronic media preserve culture in ways print media can never do. People today can reinterpret and use cultural symbolism in new temporal

Photos 5.8, 5.9 Transculturation in Mexico City. Photo 5.8: pop music icons, movie stars, and religious heroes mesh into a mosaic of wall hangings for sale. Photo 5.9: natural foods, curative herbs, vitamins, and powders vended by a recent immigrant to the city (photos by James Lull)

contiguities, greatly expanding the range of personal meanings and social uses. Mixing the traditional with the modern is fully reasonable and practical in the range of contemporary cultural possibilities. It may even be necessary. As Martín-Barbero points out, "[people] first filter and reorganize what comes from the hegemonic culture and then integrate and fuse this with what comes from their own historical memory," a process enhanced by media (1993: 74; see also Rowe and Schelling, 1991). The cultural memory of symbolic forms and communications technology is thus a basic resource for exercises of cultural programming and power.

Transculturation synthesizes new cultural genres while it breaks down traditional cultural categories. Modern communications technology facilitates the creative process. As García Canclini observes,

> technologies of reproduction allow everyone to equip their home with a repertoire of discs and cassettes that combine high culture with the popular, including those who have already synthesized many sources in the production of their works: Piazzola who mixes the tango with jazz and classical music; Caetano Veloso and Chico Buarque who have appropriated at the same time poetry of Afro-Brazilian traditions with post-Weberian experimental music. (1989: 283)

The information highway travels through contexts of both cultural production and reception as it simultaneously moves many directions in space and time.

Transculturation produces cultural hybrids – the fusing of cultural forms. Hybrid forms and genres are popular almost by definition. Consider, for example, the global flow of rap music in the 1990s. Originating in America's inner-city ghettos, rap music and hip-hop culture has travelled all over the world where it has encountered and influenced many kinds of local pop music. Some of the biggest selling Latin American pop music artists fuse rap with pop, salsa, tropical, and reggae. Mainland Chinese pop singers have rap songs in their repertoires. Christian rap is here.

The third concept, indigenization, is part of hybridization. Indigenization means that imported cultural forms take on local features. Continuing with our example, consider what happens when rap music is exported to a place like Indonesia. The unfamiliar, imported cadence and attitude of rap is appropriated by Indonesian musicians. But the sounds become indigenized at the same time. Indonesian rap is sung in local languages with lyrics that refer to local personalities, conditions, and situations. The

Photo 5.10   Hybridization. Japanese cuisine meets soul food in San Francisco (photo by James Lull)

musical hybrid is an amalgam of American black culture and Indonesian culture. But of course hybrids such as this never develop from "pure" cultural forms in the first place. American black culture has already been strongly influenced by African cultures and by European-American cultures, while Indonesian culture reflects a history of Indian subcontinental and South East Asian influences. They were hybrids themselves long before they met each other. Cultural indigenization takes place within national boundaries too. The spectacular Brazilian cultural tradition, *Carnaval*, is telecast throughout the country on the national TV system, *Globo*. But rather than imitate the famous Rio version of *Carnaval*, people throughout Brazil modify the "TV stimulus" (not only of *Carnaval*, but of national TV fare generally) by diffusing it in ways that integrate local preferences and traditions (Kottak, 1990: 174). Furthermore, the Brazilian audience, especially lower middle class, working class, and lower class viewers, definitely prefer Brazilian programs over imported television shows. This is the case in other Latin American countries too (Straubhaar, 1989). Imported television programs that succeed anywhere in the world usually resonate harmoniously with local cultural orientations or represent universal genres such as melodrama and action.

Although transculturation, hybridization, and indigenization may indeed bring about "the mutual transformation of cultures" (Rowe and Schelling, 1991: 18), the transformations often entail unequal economic power relations between the interacting cultures. The McDonald's hamburger franchise in Rio de Janeiro, for instance, promotes meal specials with titles such as "*McCarnaval*" and "*Lanche Carioca*" (the Rio resident's lunch). McDonald's, the external cultural form, has been indigenized. But to whose advantage? From McDonald's point of view, the idea is to sell more hamburgers by tapping into local culture. The Rio McDonald's may have a slightly Brazilian edge to its personality, but the local workers still scurry about for minimum wage and most of the profits end up in San Diego. The market influences the music industry this way too. When the Australian rock band Midnight Oil's videos were exported to the United States for airplay on MTV, for instance, background scenes were changed to look less Australian, more New York. We must always ask,

Photos 5.11, 5.12 Costume jewelry for Rio de Janeiro. Brazilians appropriate the Christian symbol to decorate their city and themselves, converting the cross's dominant meaning from religious to aesthetic significance (photo 5.11 by Aldo Colombo; photo 5.12 by James Lull)

therefore: on whose terms and for what purposes do cultural hybrids develop?

Reterritorialization

> Thank God for cable television! If not for cable, baseball fans in Texas would be forced to follow the [Houston] Astros and the [Dallas-based] Texas Rangers. Holy Cow! (fan letter to *The Sporting News*; the expression "Holy Cow!" is a famous line Chicago Cubs' baseball announcer Harry Caray uses on his satellite-transmitted, national cable TV broadcasts)

The sites and styles of cultural territories have changed in the modern world, but people still organize themselves culturally in order to carve out their personal identities and feel secure. No doubt, the "disembedding (lifting out) . . . of social relations from local contexts of interaction and their restructuring across indefinite spans of time and space" can be very disorienting and intimidating (Giddens, 1990: 21). But by developing new cultural territories and "re-embedding" social relations in new contexts, people can overcome the depersonalizing tendencies of modern life to find emotional relief and security (pp. 141–2). Cultural environments in which time and space acquire additional modalities need not destroy social relationships or dehumanize life in general. New ways of conceptualizing time and space can in fact provide the very basis for refashioning stable social relations (Giddens, 1991: 17).

Reterritorialization is a broad concept that embraces two coactive phenomena. It means first that the foundations of cultural territory – ways of life, artifacts, symbols, and contexts – are all open to new interpretations and understandings. Second, reterritorialization implies that culture is constantly reconstituted through social interaction, sometimes by creative uses of personal communications technology and the mass media. Cultural reterritorialization, thus, is not something done to people over which they have no control.

People everywhere continue to invent meaningful ways of living that draw from familiar anchors such as language, religion, styles of social interaction, food, and so on. These cultural elements are no longer situated solely in traditional territories of time and space. Because culture is constructed and mobile, it is also synthetic and multiple. Immigrant groups all over the world create local versions of distant cultures. But we must not think of cultural reterritorialization simply as a consequence of shifting populations. Cultural reterritorialization is part of life for people who never leave home too. Some of the most significant and vast cultural territories are mediated, symbolic lands.

Widespread access to point-to-point consumer communications technology facilitates mediated interpersonal communication helping to construct culture in new locations. People who live thousands of miles apart use telephones to nurture and expand their cultural territories. Such is the case, for example, with Taiwanese, Filipino, and Mexican immigrants living in the United States who regularly communicate with family and friends in their places of geographic origin. Communications technology greatly expands the very nature of a cultural field by facilitating social interaction that is not bound to physical space. Put another way, culture can be actively reterritorialized into new physical spaces by the ability of communications technology to facilitate social interaction that transcends physical distance.

Paul Willis (1990) prefers to call "mass" media the "cultural" media. This change in nomenclature is appropriate for several reasons. First, the original meaning of "mass media" implied that a source could "mass produce" messages to be sent to a "mass audience" in a process of "mass communication" which, in the minds of some critics, helped create a debased "mass culture." Media technology today permits wider circulation of messages than ever before. But the abundance, power, and convenience of modern communications technology have also given audiences many more choices and far greater control over reception. The choices, interpretations, and uses that people make of the mass media are cultural decisions and activities. This is true of Mexican immigrants in northern California, for instance, who watch the three Spanish-language cable TV stations in the Bay Area, listen to the many Spanish-language radio stations, rent the same video classics their friends and families view in Mexico, and buy the latest Luis Miguel pop album or Vicente Fernández ranchera LP.

At the same time American-born white kids across town lace up their Air Jordans, crank up Guns 'N Roses on their CD players, and spend hours every day playing video games. People everywhere routinely use cultural media to develop their identities, exercise their personal ambitions, and shape their social worlds.

Media imagery can also symbolically bring together people who don't know each other. "Interpretative communities" are relatively anonymous groups of people who interpret particular mediated materials with shared enthusiasm or a common viewpoint. Female readers of romance novels, regular donors to Pat Robertson's TV evangelism crusade, fans of the Grateful Dead ("Deadheads") who follow the rock group around the world, daily Rush Limbaugh listeners, and Star Trek fanatics ("Trekkies") are all interpretative communities. They are audiences defined more by their identities and discourses than by demographic similarities (see Skovmand and Schroder, 1992).

Although the media often contribute positively to cultural reterritorialization, one argument has it that symbolic reality is so pervasive and superficially appealing nowadays it has become more "real" than nature (McKibben, 1992). Mediated images reference other symbolic images so extensively that one communication theorist argues (perhaps too cynically) that we live in a "hell of mirrors" (Neiva, 1992). When media texts refer to other media texts, the process is called "intertextuality" (see Fiske, 1987, 1989, for a discussion of this). Not only texts but the media themselves are mediated. Books become films. Films become TV programs. Music becomes video clips. Photos and videotape images are reproduced in newspapers, and so on. Communications media extend the human senses (McLuhan, 1964), cultures (Lull, 1988; 1990), and each other.

Reterritorialization, therefore, is a process of active cultural selection and synthesis drawing from the familiar and the new. But creative construction of new cultural territories also involves new ways of interpreting cultural icons in processes of resignification. The entire cultural milieu, even time-honored institutions, become symbolic resources to be used in ways that differ radically from their original meanings and functions. One clear example of this is how public space and monuments are defined and used for cultural and political purposes. In the United States, huge demonstrations for minority, gay, and women's rights, for example, take place in locations that symbolize human rights and freedom – the grounds and monuments of the nation's capital, Washington, DC. The same thing happens in China. Tiananmen Square, located adjacent to the spot where the People's Republic of China was founded, has been occupied many times to demonstrate against the "people's" government. A famous monument in Mexico City dedicated to liberal reformer Benito Juárez has likewise been used by families to protest the mysterious disappearance of their kin and by women's groups to demand the right to abortion and "voluntary motherhood."[13] All these sites have great original meaning which is used ironically to speak out against policies of the governments that put them there.

Semi-public space can also be used symbolically. The great, sprawling American shopping mall, for example, is a semi-public space of unique importance in the United States, signifying another "right" Americans demand – the right to consume (to the credit card limit, in air-conditioned comfort, with plenty of free parking)! The popularity of shopping malls makes them particularly good cultural territories for public redefinition. In Santa Cruz, California, for example, gay rights activists staged a "kiss-in" in a mall to proclaim, according to the group's leaders: "We exist. Deal with it." Streets and sidewalks are other common sites of cultural transformation, and not just for symbolic political protest. In Brazil, for instance, vendors claim sidewalk space to sell a wide range of inexpensive items during the day. At night thousands of poor families sleep there. This blurring between public and private space is commonplace. Such appropriations, however, are also subject to reappropriation. During the international ecology conference in Rio in 1992, for example, the government swept vendors, families, and runaway children off the streets in order to clean up the city while foreign dignitaries were in town. Under normal circumstances, the government really has no alternative but to turn the street over to small-time merchants and poor families in order to avoid widespread civil unrest. Cultural territory thus is subject to constant appropriation and reappropriation depending on people's needs, the varieties of power they hold, and timing.

Cultural environments today are constructed of mediated and unmediated elements, of the highbrow and the popular, of the

Photos 5.13, 5.14 Appropriating public space. Photo 5.13: Chinese students hold forth at Tiananmen Square. Photo 5.14: the Benito Juárez monument in Mexico City, scene of demonstrations for many causes (photos by James Lull)

personal and the mass, of the public and the private, of the here and there, of the familiar and the strange, of yesterday, today, and tomorrow. As I hope to have shown in this chapter, people draw ambitiously from all available material and symbolic domains as they socially construct their cultural worlds. Further developing this theme, we conclude this book in the next chapter with a theoretical perspective that synthesizes the complex and contradictory forces making up the contours and formats of contemporary communication and culture.

6
Itineraries of the Everyday

We have wrestled with one central theoretical problem throughout this book. The issue in question is by no means unique to the analysis and perspective presented within these pages. In one way or another, theorists and writers from all the social sciences have long tried to understand the dynamic relation between two basic, seemingly contradictory forces: the ideological and cultural structures represented and articulated by society's political-economic-cultural elite on the one hand, and, on the other, the energy, creativity, intentionality, and transcendent ability of individual persons and subgroups to construct meaningful, enjoyable, unique identities and ways of living. As we have seen, mass media are central players within both the confining macrosocial domains and the empowering microsocial spheres. Any creditable theory must in some way account for both sides of the social power equation.

I have approached this apparent dichotomy from a perspective that emphasizes the role of mass media in modern society, patterns and processes of human communication, and the social construction of diverse cultures. We have traveled theoretical terrain that encompasses key concepts and issues from communication studies, sociology, cultural studies, political economy, psychology, and anthropology. Our analysis has considered domains of human thought and activity ranging from the specific motives of indi-

vidual persons to patterns of global human migration. We have
visited the premodern, modern, high modern, and postmodern
eras. Now, as we conclude, how do we finally explain the complex
mosaic of sociocultural forces that compete for symbolic and
cultural power in today's world?

It is surely off the mark, I believe, to regard the effects of
communications technology and the flow of symbolic imagery as
fully one-sided and exploitative in favor of dominant institutions,
ideologies, and cultures. Such a narrow perspective fails to consider the complex and indeterminate nature of symbolic interaction. I certainly agree with John B. Thompson that dominant
ideologies do in fact exist and that they can frame perceptions and
inspire interpretations that serve the general interests of dominant
social institutions (1990: 7; see also chapter 1 of this volume). But
as Thompson himself argues, ideology is "a creative and constitutive feature of social life which is [not only] sustained and reproduced, [but also] contested and transformed, through actions and
interactions which include the ongoing exchange of symbolic
forms" (p. 10). Because ideology must be represented symbolically
to be effective, its consequences cannot be confidently predicted.
We should not equate the power to expose and frame ideas with
the power to control the response. Like all symbolic displays, even
the most systematic and didactic varieties, ideologies are resources
whose significance is manifest not only through representation,
but through specific interpretations and uses. Social change, the
defining characteristic of world history, unmistakably demonstrates that ideology is negotiated and contested, not imposed and
assumed. Individual persons, social groups, nations, and cultures
should not be considered victims of dominant social forces. We
must conclude that the media/cultural imperialism thesis discussed
in the previous chapter, therefore, is not wrong but incomplete.
Furthermore, the more complex theory of ideological and cultural
hegemony – wherein institutional forces are said to converge on
behalf of the vested interests of society's political-economic elite –
is also ultimately unsatisfying. Although hegemony brilliantly
helped explain the near totalizing impact of militant European
fascism during the early twentieth century, global political and
cultural conditions differ greatly today. Theories of ideological
and cultural hegemony divide social classes too neatly and predict

their behavior with unsubstantiated certainty. Beyond this, "Not every assumption of hegemonic power by the underclass is a sign of submission and not every rejection is resistance. Not everything that comes 'from above' represents the values of the dominant class. Some aspects of popular culture respond to logics other than the logic of domination" (Martín-Barbero, 1993: 76).

The other side of the coin is popular resistance to dominant ideology and culture. But, just as social institutions including mass media cannot completely control their audiences, the autonomy and power of individuals and subjugated groups is also limited. For this reason I do not want to argue completely against the essential line of reasoning that underlies theories of imperialism or hegemony. No doubt there is more than a grain of truth to the idea that society's major ideology-producing institutions do serve in many ways to reinforce each other and reaffirm complementary modes of substantial economic, political, and cultural power. And, although people do indeed invent and reinvent ideology and culture within the situated sites and moments of everyday life, microsocial behavior does in fact often reflect the ideological and cultural preferences and limits of macrosocial structures. As our relentless critical conscience Herb Schiller argues,

> Individual expression occurs each time a person dresses, goes out for a walk, meets friends, converses, or does any of a thousand routine exercises. Expression is an inseparable part of life. It is ludicrous to imagine that individual expression can be completely managed and controlled. Yet, no matter how integral to the person, it is ultimately subject to social boundaries that are themselves changeable but always present. These limits have been created by the power formations in society, past and present. (1989: 6)

Or, as Celeste Condit points out, "We can endlessly generate studies that demonstrate that clever readers can take pleasure in reconstructing texts, but this does not certify that mass communication in general functions as a force for positive social change" (1989: 116). Even radical excorporation of cultural fragments at the microsocial level does not necessarily endure or improve things structurally.

In the midst of celebrating human initiative, resistance, creativity, and transcendence, therefore, let us not lose perspective. We have discussed in previous chapters, for instance, how young people actively construct their cultural worlds by smartly using symbolic resources at their disposal. But youth rarely resist authority at a conscious ideological level; rather, they use media resources to pass time, solve personal problems, impress their friends, declare independence from their parents and other authority figures, form and maintain personal and group identities, and so on. Similarly, the celebrated active TV viewer is not always someone who is constantly alert and resistant to the ideological content of television's messages, ever ready to reformulate the medium's apparent intended meanings or to evaluate the political and cultural consequences of viewing. In fact, mediated imagery helps create and confirm ideological and cultural motifs and categories. Routine assimilation of media message content into everyday interpersonal discourse often introduces, reinforces, and extends the dominant ideological and cultural biases contained within them. Because audience members can only select from the range of media content made available to them, they can only receive, interpret, extend, and reformulate the same images, themes, and ideas. And while the explosion of new technological forms and increased channel capacity in recent years has dramatically increased user options, the choices are still guided by sponsors. So, in one fundamental and lasting sense, mass media undeniably ground certain aspects of human experience in selected symbolic representations. Ironically, the personal, social, and cultural *uses* of media hardware and content by audiences can be at the same time some of media's most profound *effects*.

Clearly, any idea that mass media act as universal oppressors or liberators grossly distorts the communication process. Mass media can be both oppressive and liberating, even at the same moment and in the same place. The relation between complex symbolic texts and complex interpretative contexts cannot be satisfactorily explained by the common array of critical or functional theories. What we have is an example of the classic standoff between "structure" and "agency." Too much emphasis on structure (dominant ideological and cultural parameters and guidelines) exaggerates the impact of social constraint, making it appear that the worlds we live in are overwhelmingly influenced by institutions outside our control. Too much attention to agency (human volition, creativity, and transcendence) can naively overlook how dominant parameters and guidelines affect us. We must find a balance in our theory. This can best be accomplished if we recognize from the start that the forces at work here are not unrelated or necessarily conflictive. In fact, structure and agency actually help constitute each other. How can we best understand this pivotal interplay of influence?

In my view, the most far-reaching, comprehensive perspective that addresses the dilemma is Anthony Giddens' theory of *structuration* (see especially Giddens, 1984; Lull, 1992b). Structuration theory is well suited to the viewpoint on media, communication, and culture I have been developing and advocating throughout this book. Ideology, consciousness, hegemony, rules, power, culture, popular culture, media effects, the active audience, interpretation, imperialism, social institutions, technology, and globalization can all be addressed through the broad ecology of structuration theory. But while the forms and processes of modern communication are certainly relevant to the theory, Giddens has had very little to say about media technology, audiences, or culture. He does, however, accord medium-range theories of interpersonal communication, especially the dramaturgical conceptions of Erving Goffman and the ethnomethodology of Harold Garfinkel, central places in his social theory. In fact one of the true strengths of structuration theory is that it does not position the close study of face-to-face interaction outside, against, or irrelevant to analysis of social structure. It is precisely their integration that constitutes structuration. This core characteristic allows us to expand structuration theory to accommodate mass-mediated communication.

Giddens defines structure as the institutional articulation of social systems embodying rules and resources which are then "recursively implicated in social reproduction" (1984: 377). But this does not mean that social actors simply embrace and imitate dominant ideological agendas and cultural themes in their everyday interactions, thereby perpetuating conditions of their own confinement. Ideological expressions and power relations contained in and suggested by large-scale social structures, fragmented and impermanent as they are, intersect local environments, each with its own resources, relations, and rules, requiring a constant sorting out. The consequences of these meetings are not predetermined. Television's symbolic imagery, for instance, is understood and used by social actors inside their homes as TV viewers and family members, and outside the home as members of various formal and informal social groups. Each of these groups has its own interpersonal and cultural dynamics, coalitions, and hierarchies that influence how any medium's messages are interpreted and used. As Dave Morley rightly observes,

> the meanings of both texts and technologies have to be understood as emergent properties of contextualized audience practices. These practices have to been seen as situated within the facilitating and constraining microsocial environments of family and household interaction. These, in turn, must be seen as being situated in, but not necessarily determined by, those of neighborhood, economy, and culture, in which acts of consumption (of both texts and technologies) provide the articulating dimension. (1992: 195)

So, while people may intentionally select, interpret, and use media programming in clever ways socially and culturally, their selections, interpretations, and uses are profoundly influenced by their domestic relationships, by their social relationships more broadly, and by the cultural contexts in which particular social relations are embedded.

Despite all the ambiguity and richness of texts, and for all the interpretative creativity people routinely exhibit in everyday life, no semantic negotiation takes place without constraints. As we know from our discussion of ideology in chapter 1, symbolic forms all have "structural features . . . which facilitate the mobilization of meaning" (Thompson, 1990: 292). So do societies. Any interpretation made of the symbolic environment will, to some extent, reflect hierarchies represented in message structure and social structure. But how exactly do textual structure and social structure influence interpretation? We surely don't want to fall into the trap of thinking that dominant ideology, modes of industrial and message production, communications technology, or social class position dictate interpretation. A definition of structure that serves us better must account not only for constraint, consistency, and control, but also for contradiction, conflict, and transcendence. So, for example, a TV commercial directed to the

American or British middle class could certainly be perceived as relevant and attractive by the enormous target audience. But a commercial for a Japanese-made consumer item shown on television in China will likely anger and disgust the majority of state workers who, compared with their lucky peers who work in the private sector, are unable to afford it. Unequal and extremely limited economic opportunity and social mobility in China, together with systemic political repression and cultural suffocation, encourage cynical interpretations of material representations. Interpretations people make of content are not only of surface images, but also of the structures that underlie them. In order to understand how structure influences interpretation, we must also consider the wider cultural, political, and economic circumstances. Structuration theory integrates macrosocial conditions with microsocial processes, emphasizing the intentionality of social actors in the contingent reproduction of institutional values and preferred social practices. This perpetual and undestined flow of structure and agency through time makes up the intrinsic duality of structuration. Duality is the essence of the theory.

The duality embraces opposition and conflict as much as it does complementarity and accommodation. As we have seen, for example, structure is not fixed, pure, or unidirectional. As Giddens points out, overarching, dominant ideological and cultural influences enter the public sphere as *properties* of social systems, not as things in and of themselves. Although structuring properties may persist, they resemble formats, frameworks, or operating principles more than ideological or cultural entities. The structuring properties are socially produced. People inside and outside the institutions which produce them are not puppets at the end of a string complying with some agreed-upon objective. They are motivated, creative human beings who have been socialized to dominant ways of thinking but are by no means limited to these patterns. Although ideology-producing institutions do not operate in a democratic or haphazard way, they are dynamic, multivocal social formations. What the culture industries and other institutions produce is always also further subject to demands of the market.

Another key claim of structuration theory is that "structural properties of social systems do not act, or act on, anyone like forces of nature to compel him or her to behave in a particular way" (Giddens, 1984: 181). Agency militates against any cause-to-effect vision of the impact of dominant ideology and culture. We must look closely at what audiences really do. When we do, we find they interact with, interpret, edit, discuss, refute, ignore, reformulate, make fun of, use, and reuse symbolic resources in their personal and interpersonal encounters with media at the time of exposure and later. As I hope to have made abundantly clear in this book, audiences engage ideology and technology not only to comprehend, but to invent, manage, and change their living situations. The preferred readings of dominant ideological institutions (to the degree we can say that such preferences exist) never enter unproblematically into social interaction to guarantee that the dominant meanings audiences take away from their media experiences are the same ones intended by the sources. Structure, thus, is a theoretical construct representing features of impermanent, institutionally articulated, rule-governed, ideological and cultural dispositions whose actual meanings and impacts are negotiated in social production and reception.

By interpreting and using symbolic resources to their advantage, audience members "produce a margin of control – not over ownership of media, but over their social meanings" (Rowe and Schelling, 1991: 109). The very nature of communication codes and processes assures tremendous latitude in symbolic exchange. Grant McCracken offers the analogy of language to demonstrate both the power and limits of institutional power, the duality of structure, the polysemy of communication codes, and the vitality of social agency:

> Each speaker of a language is both constrained and empowered by the code that informs his language use. He or she has no choice but to accept the way in which distinctive features have been defined and combined to form phonemes. He or she has no choice but to accept the way in which the phonemes have been defined and combined to form morphemes. The creation of sentences out of morphemes is also constrained, but here the speaker enjoys a limited discretionary power and combinatorial freedom. This discretionary power increases when the speaker combines sentences into utterances. By this stage the action of compulsory rules of combination has ceased altogether. (1990: 63).

This way of thinking about communication is consistent with Chomsky's (1972) notion of generative grammar and with the dynamic view of culture present in Bourdieu's "habitus" (see chapter 3).

The cultural factor

What's missing from structuration theory that really must be addressed is the importance of culture in relation to structure and agency. Communication both constructs and is framed by culture in contexts that range from the local to the global. People interpret ideas, images, stories, and points of view in part by melding cultural memories with a cultural imagination (Martín-Barbero, 1993: 227). The mass media, of course, play a major role in this contemporary communications activity. How media content is assimilated, modified, resisted, and transformed in social intercourse demonstrates how particular relationships between structure and agency will always reflect historically situated cultural circumstances. Much of this book has been dedicated to supporting this claim.

We have several very productive theoretical initiatives on culture and symbolic interaction to further pursue. Arjun Appadurai's work on cultural globalization and Néstor García Canclini's notion of cultural hybridization have already been re-viewed in these pages (see chapter 5), as has John B. Thompson's mediazation thesis (see chapter 1). The Mexican communication theorist Jorge González (1986; 1987) has advanced an extremely interesting idea he calls "cultural fronts" (*frentes culturales*). González essentially argues that people's cultural energy is not spent in battles against media or cultural imperialism, nor are their struggles necessarily based in stresses produced by social class differences. Instead, everyday life is constructed on many levels and on many fronts that mainly concern the formation of histori-cally specific cultural identities.[1]

Cultural discourse is another prominent approach present in the theorizing of scholars such as Stuart Hall and John Fiske. Mass media institutions and technologies, Hall claims, transmit particu-lar cultural discourses that are "organized into dominant or preferred meanings" (1980: 134). But as Fiske (1987; 1989) points out, and as I have shown in a lengthy discussion of cultural power (see chapter 3), how there discourses are negotiated in social practice is not predetermined or necessarily confining.

In my comparative research on family television viewing around the world (Lull, 1988; 1990), for instance, I have promoted cultural "extension" as a useful way to think about how modern communication forms interact with social environments. In this work I suggest that family television viewing both reflects and transforms (thereby extending) culture. Again, cultural particularity is key. Family television viewing in Pakistan, for instance, differs greatly from that of Denmark; routine viewing in Venezuela does not much resemble everyday life with TV in Germany. Television viewing extends the discourses, mental orientations, and characteristic day-to-day behaviors that are the constitutive and regulative bases of culturally and historically situated social interaction (see chapter 2).

A final word

To account for the complex, interacting, often contradictory nature of media, communication, and culture we must recognize three fundamental axioms: structure is unfixed and nondetermining; symbolic messages are polysemic and multisemic; and social actors interpret and use the symbolic environment in ways that advance their personal, social, and cultural interests. We are mainly concerned with *how* culture is continually constructed in communication; the cultural disjunctures, hybrids, fronts, strategies, interventions, mediations, discourses, and extensions can all promote understanding. What we have in the end is a meshing of rule-governed environments – complex and contradictory message systems produced and distributed by social institutions that enter culturally diverse venues and communities of reception, interpretation, and use. By stressing social actors' agency in the production and reception of messages, the indeterminate character of modern communications technology and the symbolic forms they display, and the mediating influence of culture, I conclude that people's lives ultimately cannot be controlled by social forces of the right or the left. Itineraries of the everyday invariably reflect not only ideological and cultural travel agents' recommended points of interest, but those of travelers too.

Notes

Chapter 1 Ideology, Consciousness, Hegemony

1 I never realized how much I had adopted core aspects of military ideology, for example, until months after leaving military service.
2 See especially Giddens' (1984) discussion of time-space "distanciation" and time geography.
3 When the executive producer of NBC's *Today* show was asked how he planned to make a proposed Sunday version of the program a ratings success, he said only half-jokingly, "We'll just make Sunday the first day of the week."
4 It's important to realize that the military suppression of the student-worker uprising in Beijing in 1989 did not stop the Chinese revolutionary movement. It made possible the dramatic and far-reaching (if less visually spectacular) economic and cultural changes that characterize the People's Republic today.

Chapter 2 Social Rules and Power

1 I must point out that this social inversion directly involves mainly people from the lower socioeconomic classes. The vast majority of middle class and upper class Brazilians take no part in the ritual and some of them truly detest the entire thing. Many families in Rio de Janeiro escape the city during *Carnaval*. Those who stay home are

likely only to watch parts of the celebration, especially the parade, on television. For many Brazilians today, *Carnaval* has become a TV ritual.

Chapter 3 Culture and Cultural Power

1 British cultural studies theorist Paul Willis (1990) has formally confronted the privileged position of "high culture" in British society by making a government-sponsored policy recommendation to cultural authorities in England that advocates recognition and financial support for what he calls the "common culture." Willis proposes that the ways of living, aesthetics, and cultural products of working class youth should be given attention at least equal to the high-culture art forms and upper class ideologies and lifestyles that British national cultural policy normally supports. Willis cites official statistics that clearly show how much more interest people have in popular music, movies, television, and pub life, for example, than "fine arts" such as theater and ballet.

2 Pierre Bourdieu is among those who use the terms "symbolic power" and "symbolic capital" in this restricted sense. For Bourdieu, symbolic power is only available to those who "have obtained sufficient recognition to be in a position to impose recognition" (1990a: 138). Symbolic power is "nothing more than economic or cultural capital which is acknowledged and recognized" (p. 135). Social agents with this status exercise symbolic power, according to Bourdieu, by their ability to name things, which, he argues, then brings them into being. The process is similar to the "agenda setting" function of the mass media. I will argue that symbolic power should not be understood so narrowly.

   Furthermore, I frequently use the terms "symbol" and "image" in this book to refer to mediated signs in general. I fully realize this is semiotic shorthand. Icons, indices, and symbols are actually three different kinds of signs (or images) that differ according to how we infer meaning from them. Charles Peirce's theory of signs (1958) provides the basis for a social semiotics where these distinctions are of crucial theoretical import. Peirce's work has been productively applied to communication theory by Jensen (1991) and Neiva (1990; 1992).

3 "The audience" is an industry expression that should not be unproblematically taken for granted. For a lengthy critical discussion of how the commercial and public service broadcast industries

conceptualize "the audience," and what that might mean, see Ang (1991).

4 The same technique – using befuddled, clumsy white men as the butt of the joke to demonstrate the athletic prowess, creativity, and cultural power of black basketball players – has long been part of the Harlem Globetrotters' international show.

5 This advertising slogan has been widely circulated on secondary media such as tee-shirts, visors, and jackets. The slogan has also been unofficially appropriated and reworded into "Just Do Me!" and circulated via the same media.

6 "Attitude" is not just a human characteristic, according to the advertising industry. Oldsmobile introduced its 1994 model Achieva on American TV commercials with a fast-paced, exciting series of illegal and highly dangerous visual spin-outs accompanied by gravel-voiced narration claiming it's "the car with some serious attitude!"

7 One high-school teacher in Chicago found an especially effective means for punishing troublemakers at school. He formed the "Frank Sinatra Detention Club." Students required to stay after school could do nothing during those hours but sit in their chairs and listen to old Frank Sinatra records. Disobedience soon declined sharply. The musical culture gap has also been effectively manipulated by the manager of a convenience store in Sacramento, California who couldn't find a way to stop young people from loitering in the parking lot outside the store. The manager piped classical music into the lot, scaring off urban youth who previously could not even be intimidated by armed security guards. The manager joked that the only potential problem with this approach is that "next thing you know, we'll be getting senior citizens loitering out there!"

8 Some perspective on rap music must be introduced here. Many people, including leaders from the black community, believe that much rap music influences youth in a very negative, counterproductive way. One black-owned and managed Los Angeles radio station recently took off the air all songs that glorify violence, gangs, drugs, casual sex, and the denigration of women – all main themes of the genre. A serious backlash against gangsta rap in particular is now being felt.

9 The Nielsen television rating company, for instance, reports that black households in the United States watch television on average 70 hours per week, about half again as much as other viewers. Black children watch nearly two-thirds more TV than their peers. Further-

more, according to Nielsen, black viewers much prefer programs with black casts and stories.

Chapter 4 The Active Audience

1 Commercial broadcasters may not want to be held responsible for the anti-social lessons their programs teach, but they profit greatly from their claims, and their track record, about the ability of commercial announcements to teach consumer behavior that benefits their advertisers.

2 This is just what most uses and gratifications researchers say they are trying to do. But, the individual is quickly lost in uses and gratifications research and in most psychologically based studies. True, the "unit of analysis" is the individual. Questions are asked of individual persons about their personal involvements with the mass media. But each person then becomes transformed into a colorless statistic which is pushed and shoved around in various tables and graphs. The unique person becomes a standardized amount of humanity whose actions are significant only to the extent that they cluster well with others in statistical representations and comparisons. While uses and gratifications research approaches the study of mass communication by analyzing individual people, we never actually get to know them.

3 Marcuse's concept of false needs is likewise subject to criticism, especially for its elitism. Is Marcuse more qualified than anyone else to tell us what we need? John Tomlinson (1991) has written extensively and provocatively about Marcuse's position in this debate.

4 Motives differ from needs, according to Giddens, because motives imply "cognitive anticipation of a state of affairs to be realized," which needs do not (1991: 64). Giddens considers motives to be cognitive orientations that primarily facilitate a person's "ontological security" or well-being. Although Giddens furnishes a useful discussion of motive, the emphasis he places on fostering ontological security (by reducing personal anxieties) is, for me, too limiting. Motives are part of much broader cognitive activity that does not neatly gather under the umbrella of ontological security or other deficiency-reduction explanations of sociopsychological behavior.

5 Within the uses and gratifications framework, *methods* (cognitive plans and associated activities) that involve mass media are rou-

tinely termed "uses." The term "use" conflates cognition with action, thereby short-circuiting the explanatory potential of uses and gratifications research.

6   The *Mayo Clinic Family Health Book*, by the way, recommends masturbation as a normal and healthy way to release sexual tension, give yourself pleasure, savor sexual fantasies, and curb impulses to engage in "inappropriate" sexual activity.

7   I discuss the differences between (mainly American) communication science and (mainly British) cultural studies in my compendium of ethnographic studies on television audiences (Lull, 1990). Detailed histories of the development of cultural studies can be found in Brantlinger (1990) and Turner (1990).

8   But see James Curran's (1990) comments on "revisionist" audience research for a particularly forceful critique of cultural studies scholars' failure to acknowledge uses and gratifications research despite the considerable similarities in approach.

9   Such dogmatism reminds me of the attitude toward social research held by the Communist Party in the People's Republic of China. Although things are changing slightly now, for years no research on political, social, cultural, or communicational issues was undertaken in China because Communist Party officials believed that in a system where ideology and culture are thought to be effectively imposed, to problematize and study such phenomena would be redundant (see Lull, 1991: 30–4). Cultural studies' privileging of the text in cultural analysis runs the same risk.

Chapter 5   Meaning in Motion

1   The comparative analysis I present in the next few paragraphs was inspired by a lecture-discussion given by the American sociologist Stanley Aronowitz at the University of California, Santa Barbara.

2   I was teaching a course Monday nights at the State University of Rio de Janeiro at the time. One of my best students called me at home that night to say there would be no reason to come to school because absolutely no students would be there.

3   Of course this was not the first appropriation of Brazilian television for popular political purposes. Domestic fiction on Brazilian TV made statements of political resistance even during the military regime. The *telenovelas* especially have expressed progressive views on subjects such as national politics, feminism, and ecology (see Straubhaar, 1989).

4 A forerunner to Collor's political problems was the discovery by the media a few months earlier that his wife had embezzled funds from a nonprofit agency she directed. Rosane Collor made personal payments to friends and family from a welfare organization charged with improving conditions for Brazil's homeless children.

5 Piracy facilitated by easy access to tape recorders accounts for two-thirds of all pop music sold in Asia, 30 percent in Africa, 21 percent in Latin America, and about 11 percent in Canada and the United States (Frith, 1992: 72).

6 One strong example of this is how audio recording technology and contemporary musical performance styles lessen the distance between artist and fan. Many club singers and groups pack very little equipment around with them, relying only on prerecorded instrumental beds which they sing over. With no stageful of equipment or roadie rituals, distance between performer and consumer of live music is significantly reduced. Anybody can mouth the lyrics.

7 Nonetheless, many theorists and researchers believe Fiske's optimistic view hopelessly romanticizes the role of audience members in meaning construction and that his claims are not sufficiently supported with empirical evidence in any case. A particular problem is the concept of "pleasure" in interpretation as it is used by Fiske, Ang (1985), Radway (1984), Morley (1980; 1986) and other cultural studies researchers. These authors tend to "oversimplify the pleasures experienced by audience members" and thereby overstate the evidence they present in their studies (Condit, 1989: 103). Furthermore, the idea that audience members find "pleasure" by reading media texts in a resistant way certainly is not always appropriate. The feelings of people in totalitarian political states when they resist dominant ideological and cultural messages, for instance, can hardly be considered "pleasures." A Western, middle class bias permeates the discussion of pleasure in much cultural studies theorizing. We must be careful not to equate the emotional state, for example, of an American teenage girl's fascination with Madonna's rebellious image, with the feelings held by workers in China as they interpret government propaganda on the state-operated mass media.

8 A German television comedy series based on the bigoted Archie Bunker character, *Motzki*, was developed soon after the fall of the Berlin Wall. The lead character viciously ridiculed East Germans and their culture. The program provoked strong reactions from Germans throughout the uncomfortably reunified nation in the early 1990s. Both *All in the Family* and *Motzki* were originally

based on a British TV series of the 1960s and 1970s, *Till Death Us Do Part.*

9   This point must be qualified. As I pointed out in chapter 4, considerable experimental and survey research has been conducted on the question of media violence (see National Institute of Mental Health, 1982, for a thorough review of the key studies). One of the major findings within the vast body of research is that children who are predisposed to violence in some way (aggressive personalities in general, victims of abuse, frustrated as an experimental precondition) react much more aggressively to violent portrayals on television and film than their calmer peers. This well-documented finding supports the point being made here. However, it is also the case in many studies that children who are not so predisposed also react aggressively to violent programming, though the effect is considerably less strong. What I want to stress here is that at least in the case of violent TV/film and aggressive behavior among children (especially boys), the media can stimulate responses that do not necessarily reflect a predisposition on the part of the viewer.

10   I'm always impressed, for example, by how alertly and vociferously my students criticize TV commercials when I show them in class. Students' viewing of the same commercials at home would surely create a much more subdued, perhaps less critical response.

11   I want to thank the Italian semiotician Francesco Casetti for insisting on this point during our discussions at the "News of the World" conference in Perugia, Italy, in 1992.

12   García Canclini's important book *Culturas Híbridas* so far is available only in Spanish. It will soon be published in English by the University of Minnesota Press. Translations from the Spanish presented here are mine.

13   See García Canclini (1989) for a fascinating discussion of this and other examples from Mexico and Latin America.

Chapter 6   Itineraries of the Everyday

1   González' Mexican colleague Guillermo Orozco Gómez (1990; 1991) has developed a successful program of empirical research and education to help families mediate the influence of television in ways that promote national cultural goals and identities.

Glossary

active audience: A theoretical perspective claiming that audience members are not passive receivers or victims of their experiences with television and other media, but instead actively interpret and use the media in ways that benefit them.

agency: A concept promoting the idea that people are knowledgeable, capable agents of social action. Refers to the ambition, intelligence, and creativity that people bring to bear on their everyday life experiences.

agenda setting: A social science term meaning that the mass media "set the agenda" (i.e. determine the topics) for social discourse by presenting certain information (news stories, entertainment, and cultural themes) while avoiding other topics.

appropriation: Making use of something for your own purposes, sometimes in direct contradiction to its original intention.

axis: Any conceptual dimension or plane on which something is analyzed or considered.

capitalism: An economic/ideological system that relies on market forces (the relatively unfettered buying and selling of goods) rather than state planning, which is characteristic of communism.

class/social class: Groups of people categorized by their relative economic and social standing (i.e. upper class, middle class, working class, lower class).

code: A system of signs understood culturally. Language is one example.

cognition/cognitive: Emphasizes the rational, thinking dimensions of mental activity (rather than the emotional aspects). Acquiring knowledge.

commodity: Anything that is produced or offered for sale. These goods and services always have ideological origins and consequences.

communication(s): Can be understood many ways. The two most common basic definitions are (1) the transmission of information through time and space, and (2) the construction of meaning through the exchange of symbolic forms.

communication studies: An academic discipline originating in the United States of America that emphasizes the study of public discourse, language, and speech as well as interpersonal, organizational, and intercultural interaction.

consciousness: The essence or totality of attitudes, opinions, and sensitivities held by individuals or groups. It is what the articulation and spread of particular ideas produces in society.

constructivism: Social theory based on the idea that people invent their worlds through social practice and communication. This perspective differs from approaches that imply that consciousness and culture are received rather than created.

convention: A rule-governed pattern of social behavior. Conventions embody and reflect cultural orientations. They prescribe social activity as "norms."

critical theory: Various streams of social theory that call attention to the problems inherent in the economic and political structures and processes of capitalism. This intellectual tradition is typically associated with Marxist critical theory, especially as developed by the "Frankfurt School" in pre-World War II Germany, and its philosophical and political derivatives.

cultural capital: Cultural knowledge and style as resources in the formation of personal identities and the exercise of social influence.

cultural extension: The idea that modern communications media spread and amplify cultural predispositions and practices in dynamic and dialectical ways.

cultural imperialism: The critical notion that the diffusion of modern cultural artifacts, images, and styles (from dominant languages and popular music to TV sets and computer hardware) around the world is a contemporary form of cultural oppression or "imperialism." These processes favor the economic, political, and cultural interests of international superpowers such as the United States, the United Kingdom, Germany, and Japan.

cultural media: Communications technology whose message content inherently carries cultural information and biases.

cultural power: The ability to define a situation culturally. The use of symbolic cultural resources in the formation of cultural identities and the exercise of social influence.

cultural studies: A relatively recent academic discipline originating in England. Places critical emphasis on social class, gender, and race in understanding culturally-situated social practice and the distribution of power in society.

cultural territory: The geographical and symbolic spaces where culture is created through human communication.

culture: An extremely complex concept defined for our purposes as the way people live – the common values, assumptions, rules, and social practices that make up and contribute to personal and collective identity and security. Culture is a very dynamic idea, especially today, because it is constructed not only from local influences, but from symbolic representations portrayed in the mass/cultural media too.

determinism: A cause-to-effect theoretical relationship. Examples are economic determinism (social class positions develop according to a hierarchy of material relations), ideological determinism (dominant ideas necessarily overrule competing thoughts), and technological determinism (the social effects of a medium such as television are linear and predictable). For an opposing view, see "negotiation."

deterritorialization: The tearing apart of cultural structures, relationships, settings, and representations.

discourse: Most generally, the way objects or ideas are talked about publicly that gives rise to particular widespread understandings. See also "agenda setting."

disjuncture: The differences, contradictions, and counter-tendencies in culture that tend to neutralize the concentration and potency of dominant forms of political-economic power.

dominant ideology: A system of ideas that asserts, reinforces, and advances the interests of a society's elite socioeconomic group.

effects research/perspective: Empirical mass communication research and theory that emphasizes the negative or manipulative impact mass media have on audiences.

elites: Refers generally to the highest socioeconomic class in capitalist societies.

empirical research: Qualitative or quantitative social science research that depends on evidence drawn from experience, generally by observing human subjects in a systematic way. Experimental, survey, and ethnographic studies are all empirical.

empower: To engage in an activity that brings out a sense of worth, confidence, or ability in an individual or group. To enable.

ethnography: A qualitative empirical research method, grounded in anthropology, that depends on participant observation, depth interviewing, and the use of informants as primary evidence in cultural analysis.

ethnomethodology: Routine, often taken-for-granted strategies of sense-making and social behavior that people employ to construct their everyday lives.

excorporation: The process by which subordinated peoples make alternative cultural statements out of resources provided by the dominant system. For example, punks pierced their skin with safety pins to assert subcultural ideology and style.

functionalism: A controversial theory which fundamentally claims that society "functions" well as a system because various institutions (e.g. schools, political parties, mass media) help maintain social stability.

genre: A category of media fare such as "soap opera," "Tejano music," "slasher films," etc.

globalization: The flow of people, images, commodities, money, ideas, and information on a global scale, which some theorists argue is creating a homogenous world culture.

gratification: To experience deep personal satisfaction/pleasure or to greatly reduce biological or psychological deficiencies.

habitus: A system of socially-learned cultural predispositions and activities that differentiates people by their tastes and lifestyles.

hardware: Technological forms, media, or communications equipment such as television stations and sets, telephones, computers, compact disc players, newspaper presses, etc.

hegemony: A process through which dominant ideology is transmitted, consciousness is formed, and social power is exercised. The power or dominance that one social group holds over others. Rather than direct manipulation of people against their interests, hegemony depends on social actors accepting their subordinate status as normal. Ideology-dispensing institutions such as schools, government, business, and mass media reinforce each other by perpetuating the status quo as common sense.

hybridization: The fusing of cultural forms often facilitated by the flow of mass mediated imagery.

ideational image systems: Systemic forms of ideological expression that combine particular images, message structure, and preferred meanings into an integrated whole.

identity: Emphasizing the cultural aspect, this term refers to the sense of belonging, security, recognition, and importance someone can feel by being a member of a group that is bound together by common values and lifestyles.

ideology: A system of ideas expressed in communication.

image: A symbolic, often visual, display or representation of an object or idea.

image system: An ideological formation whose influence is facilitated by how the ideas are represented and framed and how they are circulated via technology and interpersonal communication.

imperialism: Originally, political–economic–cultural hegemony exercised by one nation over others. In contemporary critical theory it usually refers to "cultural imperialism" or "media imperialism," reflecting concern about how communications hardware and software are used by world superpowers to impose their political–economic–cultural values and agendas on less powerful nations and cultures.

indigenization: The process by which imported cultural materials ranging from food to architecture and popular music are adapted to local cultural conditions.

institution: Societal organizations such as public schools, political parties, prisons, and mass media industries that help regulate human behavior and, doing so, reinforce dominant ideologies and cultures.

interpersonal communication: Verbal and nonverbal interaction that takes place between two or more persons who share a code and have relatively equal opportunity to contribute to the communicative event.

interpretation: To construct meaning from symbolic representation.

logical positivism: A scientific philosophy emphasizing perception through the human senses. Originating in the natural and physical sciences, positivism has been appropriated by behaviorists and other quantitatively-oriented researchers and theorists in the social sciences in order to distance themselves from more intuitive approaches such as psychoanalysis, semiotics, cultural studies, and feminist theory.

macrosocial: Large-scale social institutions, structures, systems, contexts, collective actions, and cultural tendencies.

mainstream: Conventional, dominant sociocultural patterns.

margin/marginal: Individuals, groups, nations, and cultures who hold relatively little political–economic–cultural power.

Marxism: A socialist theory of economics and politics based on the mid-eighteenth-century writing of Karl Marx and Friedrich Engels. Marxist theory criticizes capitalism as an inherently unfair system wherein the economic elite ruthlessly exploit workers. Marx focused on economic power as the locus of social control, but later versions of Marxism emphasize the influence of ideology and culture.

mass communication: The transmission and reception of information and entertainment through media technology such as newspapers, magazines, radio, television, and film. A communication process featuring few sources, many receivers, and limited opportunity for feedback.

mass media: Communication industries and technologies that includes newspapers, magazines, radio, television, and film. The term "mass" refers to the ability of the communication technologies to send messages over broad expanses of space and time in order to reach many people.

meaning: What something signifies or represents to a person. Meaning is not inherent in symbolic forms, but is constructed by people who interpret the symbolic environment in accord with their own orientations, interests, and competencies.

media imperialism: See "imperialism."

mediational image systems: How ideology is expressed and elaborated by technological intervention and interpersonal communication.

message: The content of communication. Symbolic forms that are generally created to represent particular intentions on the part of the sender, but are open to many possible interpretations.

message system: A way of conceptualizing the totality of a medium's content as an integrated ideological whole.

method: A term that is used two ways in this book. From the sociological tradition of ethnomethodology, method refers to the particular ways people construct, make meaningful, and rationalize even the most basic actions in their everyday lives. From the perspective on audience "uses and gratifications" discussed in chapter 4, method refers to media-related strategies people use to gratify their human needs.

methodology: The strategies and procedures that social scientists use to conduct their research.

microsocial: In contrast to the overarching, structural nature of the macrosocial, this term refers to small-scale, local, intimate, technologically-unmediated social settings and relationships.

modernity: A status of economic, technological, political, and cultural development usually discussed in terms of nations. Modernity typically refers to a combination of post-industrial, consumer-oriented economic practices, a high level of technological development, some form of democratic politics, and the overall ascendancy of secular influence. The term modernity, like postmodernity, also frequently refers to a stage in world history. This use of the term is problematic, however, because many parts of the world are not yet modern or postmodern.

motive: An impulse or drive that incites human action.

multisemy: The idea that all symbolic forms not only have various possible meanings for many different people, but multiple meanings for single individuals too.

needs: According to many psychologists, needs are biological, cognitive, and emotional requirements that give direction to human behavior. By gratifying needs, people maintain their physiological and mental stability.

negotiation: The idea that the meanings of symbolic representations and cultural patterns are not determined or self evident, but subject to many possible interpretations and uses. In semiotics and cultural studies, negotiation often refers to the ways audience members interpret and use media texts like TV shows, films, or popular music. The negotiation is between the apparent intended significance of a text (representing the political–economic–cultural interests of media sources) and the construction of meaning fashioned by receiver/interpreters who act as agents for their own interests.

norm: A structured, patterned, rule-governed way of thinking and doing things that conveys an expectation of social conformity.

paradigm: A model, system, or organized perspective in academic work that advocates particular theories and research methodologies, often to the exclusion of competing approaches.

patriarchy: Social dominance of women by men.

political economy: A critical theory deriving from Marxism that claims socioeconomic elites control global communication and culture through massive political and economic influence.

polysemy: A concept from semiotics which asserts that signs (symbols, images) have many possible meanings or interpretations.

popular culture: Typically refers to commercially successful, mainstream, mass mediated cultural artifacts and personalities. Popular culture is often contrasted negatively with "high culture." For our purposes, however, the term refers to cultural experiences produced by ordinary people as originators, interpreters, and users of symbolic resources.

popular cultural capital: Means that popular symbolic resources can be used as a kind of valuable currency in social interaction.

postmodernism: A fashionable but vague and misleading term meant to describe a chaotic, fragmented, confused, groundless state of affairs in society that manifests itself in everything from interpersonal relations to art and architecture. The directionlessness and ennui of postmodernism is said to develop after a society has become fully modern. See "modernity."

preferred reading: In the parlance of cultural studies and semiotics, this refers to the way a society's dominant ideological, social, and cultural forces want audiences to interpret symbolic communications emanating from major social institutions, especially the mass media, in order for the elites to maintain their power.

reception theory/research: A mainly European approach to analyzing audiences that focuses on how people create meaning and experience in their interaction with media texts.

representation: The encoding and display of symbolic forms that reflect ideological positions.

reterritorialization: The dynamic recasting of cultural territory – often influenced by mass media – that alters traditional cultural boundaries and characteristics.

rules: The explicit codes and implicit understandings that constitute and regulate social behavior. Rules assert what is normal, acceptable, or preferred and how social interaction is to be carried out.

selectivity: Psychological processes underlying how people choose, avoid, perceive, interpret, remember, and forget symbolic imagery.

semantics/semiotics: The study of how symbolic forms (signs) are interpreted. The scientific study of meaning construction.

site: The location (physical or theoretical) where some struggle over meaning and power takes place.

social mediation: The way mass-mediated ideology is spread, reinforced, and altered through interpersonal communication.

social practice: Routine, unmediated social interaction, including verbal and nonverbal interpersonal communication.

social rules: See "rules."

social uses of media: How the form and content of mass media are used for specific purposes as resources in the construction of desired microsocial relations.

software: The content of technologically-mediated communication (e.g. TV programs, news on the radio, computer programs, etc.)

spatial consciousness: How physical distance and space is perceived, ranging in scope from the influence of telecommunications media on a global scale to the meaning of domestic and other local settings.

structure: Can refer to (1) the interrelated complex of institutions in a society or to (2) the dominant ideological themes those institutions produce.

structuration: A social theory developed by British sociologist Anthony Giddens that attempts to synthesize the apparently confining forces of "structure" with the empowering forces of "agency."

subconscious: Below or outside conscious awareness.

subculture: A group of people whose values and lifestyle differ from dominant or mainstream culture, thereby unifying the group and creating an identity for its members. Subcultures can embrace total or partial ways of life, and can oppose mainstream culture or exist alongside it as a complementary, non-resisting alternative.

subjectivity: Emphasizes personal thoughts, orientations, knowledges, and feelings as paramount in interpretation. Stands opposed to the idea that symbolic forms have "objective" referential qualities which can be understood in any uniform or determined way.

subliminal persuasion: Attempts to influence thought and action by using mediated imagery that exists below the threshold of conscious perception. Appeals to subconscious desires.

symbol: As used in this book, a general term referring to any image or representation that stands for something else.

symbolic power: The use of symbolic forms, especially media imagery, to influence the course of social action and events.

taste culture: A sociological concept, depending in part on social class position, that describes how people can be grouped according to their cultural preferences or "tastes."

technological mediation: The intervention of communications technology in social interaction, particularly the influence of mass media on the diffusion of ideology.

temporal consciousness: How time is perceived. For purposes here, how the mass media alter conceptions of time.

text: The content of symbolic communication, often used in terms of what the mass media (and not just the print media) present. A text, therefore, can be a TV program, movie, CD-Rom, or rock song, among many other possibilities.

Third World: The less developed parts of the world, especially Africa, Latin America, and parts of Asia.

transculturation: A process by which a cultural form (e.g. language, food, music) moves from one physical location to another where it interacts with and influences the local forms (languages, food, music, etc.) and produces new cultural hybrids.

uses and gratifications: A theoretical development in communication studies associated with the idea that media audiences are "active."

According to this perspective, people use the media and other sociocultural resources to gratify basic human needs.

value: A constellation of deeply-held, enduring attitudes, beliefs, and predispositions that reflect the ideological and cultural orientations of an individual or group of people.

wants: In contrast to "needs," which are core biological and psychological states said to motivate human behavior, wants are the less weighty desires people have.

References

Alexander, J.C. and Seidman, S. (eds) (1990). *Culture and Society: Contemporary Debates*. Cambridge, UK: Cambridge University Press.

Ang, I. (1985). *Watching Dallas: Soap Opera and the Melodramatic Imagination*. London: Routledge.

Ang, I. (1991). *Desperately Seeking the Audience*. London: Routledge.

Appadurai, A. (1990). Disjuncture and difference in the global cultural economy. In M. Featherstone (ed.), *Global Culture: Nationalism, Globalization, and Modernity*. London: Sage.

Archer, M. (1990). Theory, culture and post-industrial society. In M. Featherstone (ed.), *Global Culture: Nationalism, Globalization, and Modernity*. London: Sage.

Bagdikian, B. (1988). *The Media Monopoly*. Boston: Beacon Press.

Barrios, L. (1988). Television, *telenovelas*, and family life in Venezuela. In J. Lull (ed.), *World Families Watch Television*. Newbury Park, CA: Sage.

Bauman, Z. (1989). *Legislators and Interpreters*. Cambridge, UK: Polity Press.

Bausinger, H. (1984). Media, technology, and everyday life. *Media, Culture and Society*, 6, 340–52.

Behl, N. (1988). Equalizing status: television and tradition in an Indian village. In J. Lull (ed.), *World Families Watch Television*. Newbury Park, CA: Sage.

Berelson, B. (1949). What "missing the newspaper" means. In P.F.

Lazarsfeld and F.N. Stanton (eds), *Communications Research, 1948–49*. New York: Duell, Sloan, and Pearce.

Blumler, J.G. and Katz, E. (1974). *The Uses of Mass Communication: Current Perspectives on Gratifications Research*. Beverly Hills, CA: Sage.

Boggs, C. (1976). *Gramsci's Marxism*. London: Pluto Press.

Bouissac, P. (1976). *Circus and Culture: A Semiotic Approach*. Bloomington, IN: Indiana University Press.

Bourdieu, P. (1984). *Distinction: A Social Critique of the Judgement of Taste*. Cambridge, MA: Harvard University Press.

Bourdieu, P. (1990a). *In Other Words: Essays Toward a Reflexive Sociology*. Cambridge, UK: Polity Press.

Bourdieu, P. (1990b). *The Logic of Practice*. Cambridge, UK: Polity Press.

Bourdieu, P. (1993). *The Field of Cultural Production*. Cambridge, UK: Polity Press.

Brantlinger, P. (1990). *Crusoe's Footprints: Cultural Studies in Britain and America*. New York: Routledge.

Chomsky, N. (1972). *Language and Mind*. New York: Harcourt, Brace, Jovanovich.

Cohen, Y. (1989). *The Manipulation of Consent: The State and Working Class Consciousness in Brazil*. Pittsburgh, PA: University of Pittsburgh Press.

Collett, P. (1977). The rules of conduct. In P. Collett (ed.), *Social Rules and Social Behavior*. Totowa, NJ: Rowman and Littlefield.

Condit, C. (1989). The rhetorical limits of polysemy. *Critical Studies in Mass Communication*, 6, 103–22.

Cooper, E. and Jahoda, M. (1947). The evasion of propaganda: how prejudiced people respond to anti-prejudice propaganda. *Journal of Psychology*, 23, 15–25.

Curran, J. (1990). The new revisionism in mass communication research: a reappraisal. *European Journal of Communications*, 5, 135–64.

Cushman, D. and Whiting, G.C. (1972). An approach to communication theory: toward consensus on rules. *Journal of Communication*, 24, 30–45.

DaMatta, R. (1991). *Carnivals, Rogues, and Heroes: An Interpretation of the Brazilian Dilemma*. Notre Dame, IN: University of Notre Dame Press.

Dorfman, A. and Mattelart, A. (1972). *Para Leer al Pato Donald: Comunicación de Masa y Colonialismo*. Mexico City: Siglo XXI.

Dunnett, P. (1990). *The World Television Industry*. New York: Routledge.

Edgerton, R.B. (1985). *Rules, Exceptions, and Social Order*. Berkeley, CA: University of California Press.

Elliott, P. (1974). Uses and gratifications research: a critique and a sociological alternative. In J.G. Blumler and E. Katz (eds), *The Uses of Mass Communications: Current Perspectives on Gratifications Research*. Beverly Hills, CA: Sage.

Erikson, E. (1982). *The Life Cycle Completed*. New York: Norton.

Ewen, S. (1976). *Captains of Consciousness*. New York: McGraw-Hill.

Featherstone, M. (1990). Global culture: an introduction. In M. Featherstone (ed.), *Global Culture: Nationalism, Globalization, and Modernity*. London: Sage.

Ferguson, M. (1989). *Public Communication*. London: Sage.

Fiske, J. (1987). *Television Culture*. London: Routledge.

Fiske, J. (1989). *Understanding Popular Culture*. Boston: Unwin Hyman.

Fiske, J. (1993). *Power Plays, Power Works*. London: Verso.

Frith, S. (1992). The industrialization of popular music. In J. Lull (ed.), *Popular Music and Communication*. Newbury Park, CA: Sage.

Gans, H. (1962). *The Urban Villagers*. New York: Free Press.

Gans, H. (1974). *Popular Culture and High Culture*. New York: Basic Books.

García Canclini, N. (1989). *Culturas Híbridas: Estrategias para Entrar y Salir de la Modernidad*. Mexico City: Grijalbo.

Garfinkel, H. (1967). *Studies in Ethnomethodology*. Englewood Cliffs, NJ: Prentice-Hall. (1984) Cambridge, UK: Polity Press.

Geertz, C. (1973). *The Interpretation of Cultures*. New York: Basic Books.

Geertz, C. (1983). *Local Knowledge*. New York: Basic Books.

Gerbner, G. (1973). Cultural indicators: the third voice. In G. Gerbner, L. Gross, and W. Melody (eds), *Communications Technology and Social Policy*. New York: Wiley.

Gerbner, G. and Gross, L. (1976). Living with television: the violence profile. *Journal of Communication*, 26, 173–99.

Giddens, A. (1984). *The Constitution of Society*. Cambridge, UK: Polity Press.

Giddens, A. (1990). *The Consequences of Modernity*. Stanford, CA: Stanford University Press. (1991) Cambridge, UK: Polity Press.

Giddens, A. (1991). *Modernity and Self-Identity: Self and Society in the Late Modern Age*. Cambridge, UK: Polity Press.

Gitlin, T. (1979). Prime-time ideology: the hegemonic process in television entertainment. *Social Problems*, 26, 251–66.

Goffman, E. (1959). *The Presentation of the Self in Everyday Life*. New York: Doubleday .

Goffman, E. (1963). *Behavior in Public Places.* New York: Free Press.

Goffman, E. (1967). *Interaction Ritual.* New York: Anchor.

Goffman, E. (1969). *Strategic Interaction.* Philadelphia: University of Pennsylvania Press.

González, J. (1986). *Culturas.* Colima, Mexico: Universidad de Colima.

González, J. (1987). Los frentes culturales: culturas, mapas, poderes, y luchas por las definiciones legítimas de los sentidos sociales de la vida. In *Estudios Sobre las Culturas Contemporaneous*, 1, 5–41.

Gramsci, A. (1971). *Selections from the Prison Notebooks.* New York: International Publishers.

Gramsci, A. (1973). *Letters from Prison.* New York: Harper and Row.

Gramsci, A. (1978). *Selections from Cultural Writings.* Cambridge, MA: Harvard University Press.

Hall, S. (1977). Culture, media, and the "ideological effect." In J. Curran, M. Gurevitch, and J. Woollacott (eds), *Mass Communication and Society.* London: Edward Arnold.

Hall, S. (1980). Encoding/decoding. In S. Hall, D. Hobson, D. Lowe, and P. Willis (eds), *Culture, Media, Language.* London: Hutchinson.

Hall, S. (1985). Master's session. International Communication Association. Honolulu, Hawaii.

Hamm, C. (1983). *Music in the New World.* New York: Norton.

Hannerz, U. (1969). *Soulside: Inquiries into Ghetto Culture and Community.* New York: Columbia University Press.

Hannerz, U. (1990). Cosmopolitans and locals in world culture. In M. Featherstone (ed.), *Global Culture: Nationalism, Globalization, and Modernity.* London: Sage.

Harré, R., Clarke, D., and De Carlo, N. (1985). *Motives and Mechanisms: An Introduction to the Psychology of Action.* London: Routledge.

Harvey, P. (1989). *The Condition of Postmodernity.* Oxford: Basil Blackwell.

Hastorf, A. and Cantril, H. (1954). They saw a game: a case study. *Journal of Abnormal and Social Psychology*, 49, 129–34.

Hebdige, D. (1979). *Subculture: The Meaning of Style.* London: Methuen.

Herzog, H. (1944). What do we really know about daytime serial listeners? In P.F. Lazarsfeld and F.N. Stanton (eds), *Radio Research, 1942–43.* New York: Duell, Sloan, and Pearce.

Horton, D. and Wohl, R. (1956). Mass communication and para-social interaction. *Psychiatry*, 19, 215–29.

Innis, H. (1950). *Empire and Communication.* Oxford: Oxford University Press.

Innis, H. (1951). *The Bias of Communication*. Toronto: University of Toronto Press.

Innis, H. (1952). *Changing Concepts of Time*. Toronto: University of Toronto Press.

Jensen, J. (1990). *Redeeming Modernity: Contradictions in Media Criticism*. Newbury Park, CA: Sage.

Jensen, K.B. (1991). When is meaning? Communication theory, pragmatism, and mass media reception. *Communication Yearbook 14*. Newbury Park, CA: Sage.

Jensen, K.B. and Jankowski, N. (eds) (1991). *A Handbook of Qualitative Methodologies for Mass Communication Research*. London: Routledge.

Johnson, M. (1987). *The Body in the Mind: The Bodily Basis of Meaning, Imagination, and Reason*. Chicago: The University of Chicago Press.

Katz, E. (1977). Looking for trouble: social research on broadcasting. Presentation made to British Broadcasting Corporation, London.

Katz, E., Blumler, J., and Gurevitch, M. (1974). Utilization of mass communication by the individual. In J. Blumler and E. Katz (eds), *The Uses of Mass Communications: Current Perspectives on Gratifications Research*. Newbury Park, CA: Sage.

Key, W.B. (1973). *Subliminal Seduction*. New York: Signet.

Key, W.B. (1976). *Media Sexploitation*. Englewood Cliffs, NJ: Prentice-Hall.

Key, W.B. (1980). *The Clam Plate Orgy and Other Subliminals the Media Use to Manipulate Your Behavior*. Englewood Cliffs, NJ: Prentice-Hall.

Klapper, J. (1960). *The Effects of Mass Communication*. New York: Free Press.

Kottak, C. (1990). *Prime-Time Society: An Anthropological Analysis of Television and Culture*. Belmont, CA: Wadsworth.

Kratochwil, F. (1989). *Rules, Norms, and Decisions*. Cambridge, UK: Cambridge University Press.

Laswell, H.D. (1948). The structure and function of communication in society. In L. Bryson (ed.), *The Communication of Ideas*. New York: Harper.

Lewis, G. (1992). Who do you love? The dimensions of musical taste. In J. Lull (ed.), *Popular Music and Communication*. Newbury Park, CA: Sage.

Liebes, T. and Katz, E. (1990). *The Export of Meaning*. New York: Oxford University Press. 2nd edn (1993) Cambridge, UK: Polity Press; Cambridge, MA: Blackwell.

Lindlof, T., Shatzer, M., and Wilkinson, D. (1988). Accommodation of video and television in the American family. In J. Lull (ed.), *World Families Watch Television*. Newbury Park, CA: Sage.

Lindsay, R. (1977). Rules as a bridge between speech and action. In P. Collett (ed.), *Social Rules and Social Behavior*. Totowa, NJ: Rowman and Littlefield.

Lull, J. (ed.) (1988). *World Families Watch Television*. Newbury Park, CA: Sage.

Lull, J. (1990). *Inside Family Viewing: Ethnographic Research on Television's Audiences*. London: Routledge.

Lull, J. (1991). *China Turned On: Television, Reform, and Resistance*. London: Routledge.

Lull, J. (ed.) (1992a). *Popular Music and Communication*. Newbury Park, CA: Sage.

Lull, J. (1992b). La estructuración de las audiencias masivas. *Día Logos*, 32, 50–7.

Lull, J. and Wallis, R. (1992). The beat of West Vietnam. In J. Lull (ed.), *Popular Music and Communication*. Newbury Park, CA: Sage.

MacBride, S. (1980). *Many Voices, One World: Communication and Society Today and Tomorrow*. New York: UNESCO.

Mander, J. (1977). *Four Arguments for the Elimination of Television*. New York: Morrow.

Marcuse, H. (1964). *One Dimensional Man*. Boston: Beacon Press.

Martín-Barbero, J. (1993). *Communication, Culture and Hegemony*. Newbury Park, CA: Sage.

Maslow, A.H. (1954). *Motivation and Personality*. New York: Harper.

Maslow, A.H. (1962). *Toward a Psychology of Being*. Princeton, NJ: Van Nostrand.

McCracken, G. (1990). *Culture and Consumption: New Approaches to the Symbolic Character of Consumer Goods and Activities*. Bloomington, IN: Indiana University Press.

McDonagh, E.C. (1950). Television and the family. *Sociology and Social Research*, 35, 113–22.

McKibben, B. (1992). *The Age of Missing Information*. New York: Penguin.

McLuhan, M. (1962). *The Gutenberg Galaxy: The Making of Typographic Man*. Toronto: Toronto University Press.

McLuhan, M. (1964). *Understanding Media: The Extensions of Man*. New York: McGraw-Hill.

McLuhan, M. and Fiore, Q. (1967). *The Medium is the Massage*. New York: Bantam.

McQuail, D., Blumler, J.G., and Brown, J.R. (1972). The television audience: a revised perspective. In D. McQuail (ed.), *Sociology of Mass Communication*. Harmondsworth, UK: Penguin.

McQuail, D. and Gurevitch, M. (1974). Explaining audience behavior: three approaches considered. In J.G. Blumler and E. Katz (eds), *The Uses of Mass Communications: Current Perspectives on Gratifications Research*. Beverly Hills, CA: Sage.

Mendelsohn, H. (1964). Listening to radio. In L.A. Dexter and D.M. White (eds), *People, Society and Mass Communications*. Glencoe: Free Press.

Merton, R. (1957). *Social Theory and Social Structure*. New York: Free Press.

Meyrowitz, J. (1985). *No Sense of Place: The Impact of Electronic Media on Social Behavior*. New York: Oxford University Press.

Morley, D. (1980). *The "Nationwide" Audience*. London: British Film Institute .

Morley, D. (1986). *Family Television: Cultural Power and Domestic Leisure*. London: Routledge.

Morley, D. (1988). Domestic relations. The framework of family viewing in Great Britain. In J. Lull (ed.), *World Families Watch Television*. Newbury Park, CA: Sage.

Morley, D. (1991). When the global meets the local: notes from the sitting room. *Screen*, 32, 1–15.

Morley, D. (1992). *Television, Audiences, and Cultural Studies*. London: Routledge.

National Institute of Mental Health (1982). *Television and Behavior: Ten Years of Scientific Progress and Implications for the Eighties*. Washington, DC: US Government Printing Office.

Neiva, E. (1990). *Comunicação: Teoria e Prática Social*. São Paulo: Editora Brasiliense.

Neiva, E. (1992). *Um Inferno de Espelhos: Comuniçacão, Cultura, e Mundo Natural*. Rio de Janeiro: Rio Fundo Editora.

Newcomb, H. and Hirsch, P. (1987). Television as a cultural forum. In H. Newcomb (ed.), *Television: The Critical View*. New York: Oxford University Press.

Nordenstreng, K. (1977). From mass media to mass consciousness. In G. Gerbner (ed.), *Mass Media Policies in Changing Cultures*. New York: Wiley.

Orozco Gómez, G. (ed.) (1990). *La Comunicación desde las Prácticas Sociales: Reflexiones en Torno a su Investigación*. Mexico City: Universidad Iberoamericana.

Orozco Gómez, G. (1991). La audiencia en frente de la pantalla. *Día Logos*, 30, 55–63.

Peirce, C.S. (1958). *The Collected Papers*. Cambridge, MA: Harvard University Press.

Postman, N. (1984). *Amusing Ourselves to Death*. New York: Penguin.

Quine, W. (1972). Methodological reflections on current linguistic theory. In D. Harman and G. Davidson (eds), *Semantics of Natural Language*. Dordrecht: D. Reidel.

Radway, J. (1984). *Reading the Romance: Feminism and the Representation of Women in Popular Culture*. Chapel Hill, NC: University of North Carolina Press.

Real, M. (1989). *Super Media: A Cultural Studies Approach*. Newbury Park, CA: Sage.

Riley, M.W. and Riley, J.W. (1951). A sociological approach to communication research. *Public Opinion Quarterly*, 15, 444–60.

Rogge, J.-U. and Jensen, K. (1988). Everyday life and television in Germany: an empathic-interpretative perspective on the family as a system. In J. Lull (ed.), *World Families Watch Television*. Newbury Park, CA: Sage.

Rosengren, K.E. (1974). Uses and gratifications: a paradigm outlined. In J.G. Blumler and E. Katz (eds), *The Uses of Mass Communications: Perspectives on Gratifications Research*. Beverly Hills, CA: Sage.

Rowe, W. and Schelling, V. (1991). *Memory and Modernity: Popular Culture in Latin America*. London: Verso.

Samuels, F. (1984). *Human Needs and Behavior*. Cambridge, MA: Schnenkman.

Sassoon, A.S. (1980). *Gramsci's Politics*. New York: St Martin's Press.

Schiller, H.I. (1969). *Mass Communications and American Empire*. Boston: Beacon Press.

Schiller, H.I. (1973). *The Mind Managers*. Boston: Beacon Press.

Schiller, H.I. (1976). *Communication and Cultural Domination*. White Plains, NY: International Arts and Sciences Press.

Schiller, H.I. (1989). *Culture, Inc.: The Corporate Takeover of Public Expression*. New York: Oxford University Press.

Schiller, H.I. (1991). Not yet the post-imperialist era. *Critical Studies in Mass Communication*, 8, 13–28.

Schramm, W., Lyle, J., and Parker, E.B. (1961). *Television in the Lives of Our Children*. Stanford, CA: Stanford University Press.

Schwichtenberg, C. (1993). *The Madonna Connection*. Boulder, CO: Westview Press.

Shimanoff, S. (1980). *Communication Rules*. Beverly Hills, CA: Sage.

Simon, R. (1982). *Gramsci's Political Thought*. London: Lawrence and Wishart.

Skovmand, M. and Schroder, K. (1992). *Media Cultures: Reappraising Transnational Media*. London: Routledge.

Smith, A. (1990). Towards a global culture? In M. Featherstone (ed.), *Global Culture: Nationalism, Globalization, and Modernity*. London: Sage.

Straubhaar, J. (1989). Mass communication and the elites. In M.L. Conniff and F.D. McCann (eds), *Modern Brazil: Elites and Masses in Historical Perspective*. Lincoln, NE: University of Nebraska Press.

Straubhaar, J. (1991). Beyond media imperialism: asymmetrical interdependence and cultural proximity. *Critical Studies in Mass Communication*, 8, 39–59.

Suchman, E. (1942). An invitation to music. In P.F. Lazarsfeld and F.N. Stanton (eds), *Radio Research, 1941*. New York: Duell, Sloan, and Pearce.

Swidler, A. (1986). Culture in action: symbols and strategies. *American Sociological Review*, 51, 273–86.

Szemere, A. (1985). Pop music in Hungary. *Communication Research*, 12, 401–11.

Thompson, J.B. (1990). *Ideology and Modern Culture*. Cambridge, UK: Polity Press.

Thompson, J.B. (1994). Social theory and the media. In D. Crowley and D. Mitchell (eds), *Communication Theory Today*. Cambridge, UK: Polity Press.

Tomlinson, J. (1991). *Cultural Imperialism*. Baltimore: The Johns Hopkins University Press.

Tufte, T. (1992). Daily life and *telenovelas*: an ethnographic study of Brazilian women's use of *telenovelas*. Presented to the International Association for Mass Communication Research, Guaruja, Brazil.

Turner, G. (1990). *British Cultural Studies: An Introduction*. Boston: Unwin Hyman.

Vidmar, N. and Rokeach, M. (1974). Archie Bunker's bigotry: a study in selective perception and exposure. *Journal of Communication*, 24, 36–47.

Wicke, P. (1992). The role of rock music in the political disintegration of East Germany. In J. Lull (ed.), *Popular Music and Communication*. Newbury Park, CA: Sage.

Williams, R. (1962). *The Long Revolution*. New York: Columbia University Press.

Williams, R. (1975). *Television: Technology and Cultural Form*. New York: Schocken.

Williams, R. (1976). *Key Words: A Vocabulary of Culture and Society.* New York: Oxford University Press.

Willis, P. (1990). *Common Culture: Symbolic Work at Play in the Everyday Cultures of the Young.* Boulder, CO: Westview Press.

Wright, C.R. (1960). Functional analysis and mass communications. *Public Opinion Quarterly,* 4, 605–20.

Wright, C.R. (1975). *Mass Communication: A Sociological Perspective.* New York: Random House.

Index